*The
Connell Guide
to*

The French Revolution

---

*by
David Andress*

Contents

A rough outline	1
Why has the French Revolution caused so much argument?	15
Pre-revolution	**19**
What caused the French Revolution?	19
How did the changing political culture breed revolution?	21
Why was France in such bad shape?	23
What were the main obstacles to reform?	25
Why was the hierarchical society of the Old Regime so hard to change?	29
How did the political culture enforce the social structure?	32
How effective was the censorship on which the "system" depended?	36
Revolution	**41**
How did men and women of the old order become revolutionaries?	41
How did French society respond to the calling of the Estates-General?	43
How significant were the popular uprisings of 1789?	48
Why did revolutionary politics become a spiral of violence?	54
Why was the Revolution seen as an attack on religion?	56
What was the effect of suspicion and inflamed passion on both sides?	60
How did a revolutionary political culture develop?	63
Why were the French so terrified of political dissent?	71
Who were the Jacobins?	75
Why was the language of the revolution so extreme?	78
Who were the "sans-culottes"?	83

The Terror	**85**
How many people were actually executed?	85
Can the violence be blamed on the bloodthirsty crowd?	88
What role did Robespierre play?	91
Why is the pace of events so significant?	96

After The Terror	**98**
Did the "real" revolution end in 1794?	98
Why was there a revival of ideological conflict after Thermidor?	101
What did the Directory actually achieve?	103
How did the Directory endure for four years?	106
Where did Bonaparte emerge from, and how did he rise so fast?	108

Conclusion	**115**

NOTES

The mind of the King	*27*
Rousseau's legacy	*39*
Fallen idols No.1: The Marquis de Lafayette	*45*
Fallen idols No.2: Jacques-Pierre Brissot	*63*
Ten facts about the French Revolution	*67*
Women and the Revolution	*71*
Fallen idols No.3: Georges Jacques Danton	*77*
Endnotes	*122*
Glossary	*125*
Further Reading	*129*

A rough outline

1763

In 1763, France lost most of its overseas territory as part of the disastrous end of the Seven Years' War.*
With the state's debts hugely increased by military costs, government ministers spent the next 15 years struggling to impose new taxes on the privileged social elite, and generally failing. Participation in the American War of Independence was even more costly, and by the late 1780s the need for structural reform of state finances had become critical.

1787-8

In 1787, finance minister Charles Alexandre de Calonne brought together an Assembly of Notables – 144 leading noble figures – to try to win agreement for new taxes and other changes. They rejected his case. A year of institutional struggles followed, and in the second half of 1788 the crown had to agree to summon an Estates-General, France's medieval "parliament", which had not met since 1614.

The Estates-General was an elected body, and

* All highlighted words and phrases are explained in the glossary on p.125

during the elections cahiers de doléances, or registers of grievance, were drawn up by every village and town. These revealed an enormous appetite for changing not just the tax system but the structure of social privileges that gave the elite much of its power, and for making representative institutions permanent.

1789

When the Estates-General met at Versailles in May 1789, the conflict between the commoners of the "Third Estate" and the noble "Second Estate" became the key issue: in June the Third Estate struck out, renaming itself the "National Assembly" and proclaiming it would give France a new constitution.

In July the royal court decided this defiance was too much. But when it tried to isolate and gain control of the Assembly, Paris erupted with popular resistance. Fearing a military attack on the city, tens of thousands armed themselves, and on 14 July stormed the fortress of the Bastille in the east of the city to secure its huge stock of gunpowder.

Louis XVI was forced to make peace with the Assembly. For a few weeks, a spirit of unity prevailed, and, spurred by news of widespread rural unrest, the Assembly agreed on 4 August to abolish many categories of social and taxation privileges, creating a united body of citizens. Later in the month they sought to enshrine their principles by drafting the *Declaration of the Rights of Man and the Citizen.*

Over the next two years, the Assembly gradually wrote a new charter for the "constitutional monarchy" they were creating. Meanwhile, dissenting nobles formed increasingly violent plans for resistance, often in alliance with the *émigrés* – opponents of reform who had emigrated across the frontiers of France.

1790

The end of privilege turned out to be complicated: many peasants felt it did not leave them any better off. The faithful were troubled by changes to the Catholic Church. The state had confiscated the Church's massive property holdings as security for its debts, and now sought to liquidate some of these assets. Violent resistance became common.

> *Meanwhile, revolutionary politics was developing its own language and practices, from an explosive growth in a free press, to the formation of political clubs. Demands to act against the "aristocratic" and "counter-revolutionary" threat became increasingly radical. Democratic elections for every post from village mayor to district judge entrenched a new bottom-up culture of politics.*

1791

Louis XVI seemed to have accepted the Revolution, but the truth was shockingly revealed in June 1791 when he tried to escape from Paris to the frontiers with his family. Recaptured at Varennes, he agreed with the Assembly's leadership to pretend he had been taken from the capital against his will – because they could not imagine how to secure the country's future without a monarch.

In the autumn, new elections produced a new Legislative Assembly, staffed by men largely drawn from the new patriotic culture of the revolution. Radical "Brissotin" leaders (so-called after Jacques-Pierre Brissot) quickly emerged, concentrating their efforts on the continuing threat of the *émigrés* (now including both of the king's brothers), and promoting war against the powers that sheltered them – particularly Austria. Soon more conservative revolutionary leaders joined this aggressive patriotic militarism, seeing war as a path to national unity.

1792

The royal family also came out in favour of war, but plotted secretly to profit from defeat by recalling the French to subordination. Only a few ultra-radicals, notably Maximilien Robespierre, recognised this as dangerous possibility, and in April 1792, war was declared on Austria, and shortly afterwards on Prussia.

> *War was disastrous. A wave of defeats was followed by the real threat of invasion. The Brissotin leadership was trapped between a rising wave of patriotic republicanism and their belief that to overthrow the monarchy would bring chaotic and total defeat.*

Strong radical forces rallied in Paris, and on 10th August 1792 forced the king to step down. Republican political forces then purged local government, arrested "suspect" nobles and priests, and co-ordinated elections for a "National Convention" to write a new constitution.

Meanwhile, enemy forces approached, capturing Verdun, the last fortified point before Paris, at the start of September. Radicals in Paris feared a counter-revolutionary uprising in the overcrowded prisons and between 2nd and 5th September killed more than 1,000 inmates.

The Brissotins (now often called "Girondins") and the more radical "Montagnards" confronted each other in the new Convention in the shadow of this massacre, each seeing the other as a dangerous threat. French armies, meanwhile, saved Paris from attack with a victory against the Prussians at Valmy on 20th September.

1793

Until the end of 1792, the Convention was divided over the fate of the king. In January 1793, after a lengthy trial, he was found guilty unanimously, but condemned to death by only a narrow majority. He was executed by guillotine on 21st January.

The spring of 1793 was marked by an expansion of the war. Britain, Spain and the Italian states were drawn in. France was committed to fighting not only on all its land frontiers but also on the high seas and in its remaining colonies. As part of the war effort, local quotas for conscription were imposed, surveillance committees were established to watch for traitors, and a Revolutionary Tribunal was created to judge political crimes. Thus the mechanisms of "the Terror" began to take shape.

While doing all this, the Convention also tore itself apart. Girondins and Montagnards, the latter supported by so-called "sans-culotte" ultra-radicals, denounced each other, sometimes even coming to blows. In this context, further betrayal erupted: in the north-west, there were massive insurrections against conscription. In the Vendée region these coalesced into a "Royal and Catholic" army of rebels.

In late May 1793, Parisian sans-culotte leaders purged the Convention, mobilising massive forces to intimidate it into expelling around two dozen Girondins. At almost the same moment, Girondin sympathisers in Lyon and Marseille rebelled against aggressive Montagnard emissaries and their local agents. Within weeks, a civil war between these two forces overlay all the other conflicts already threatening to tear France apart.

The Convention's Committee of Public Safety, charged with overseeing the government, was reorganised in July 1793. Robespierre joined it to campaign for patriotic unity and sacrifice, building on his reputation for incorruptibility. Meanwhile, despite celebrating the completion of a new democratic constitution with a festival on 10th August, the Convention declined to call new elections, claiming the conditions were too dangerous.

In Paris, the Montagnard-dominated Convention faced pressure from the sans-culotte movement that claimed to represent the common people, starving thanks to "counter-revolutionary" hoarding. This pressure helped to produce new laws: the levée en masse (a Mass Levy committing the whole population to the war effort); the Law of Suspects, ultimately placing tens of thousands in detention; and the General Maximum, a system of price controls that spread a new bureaucracy across the country. New "revolutionary armies" formed of sans-culotte militants were recruited, not to fight on the frontiers, but to hunt down hoarders.

The autumn of 1793 saw the internal military situation come under control – both Vendée rebels and pro-Girondin forces were crushed – while combat on the frontiers was at least stabilised. In Paris, the Girondin leadership, Marie-Antoinette, and a series of other notable figures were given show trials at the Revolutionary Tribunal and sent to the guillotine.

These months also saw the first serious divisions amongst the Montagnards. While some advocated a "de-Christianising" attack on all faith as part of an uncompromising approach, others argued for a relaxation of attacks on internal treachery, and pursuit of negotiated peace. There were rumours, and some evidence, of real corruption in both camps. By the end of the year, a new wave of official purging of all public offices was decreed, spreading further fear and division.

1794

During the winter of 1793/94, the practical measures of mobilisation put in place enabled the successful raising, arming and training of massive new armies, approaching a million men, and in the spring these began successful offensive action on all fronts.

At the same time, the politics of the Terror began to consume the Montagnard leadership. Real evidence of corruption mingled with rumours and fabrications. The sans-culotte leadership was purged first in March 1794, shutting down independent radical politics in the capital; then the peace faction was denounced, tried, and executed, all in the space of a few days.

> *Robespierre was only one of those involved in these decisions, but he came to be seen as the leader of the intensifying political cannibalism. By the early summer, as the Convention pressed on with grand plans for the cultural regeneration of the Republic, it was also approving new, faster trials and mass-executions.*

With success on the battle-front, the pressure to purge seemed increasingly detached from reality, more like a "Robespierrist" plot to seize power. On 9 Thermidor (or 27th July), all the many Montagnards Robespierre was threatening in the Convention rallied to send him, four other Convention members, and about 100 of their supporters, to the guillotine.[1]

After Thermidor the Convention continued in office for another 15 months. While some had seen Robespierre's fall as a chance to "save" radical republicanism, it soon became clear that a relaxation of terror had let more conservative forces back into politics. The political pendulum swung

Opposite: Portrait of Maximilien Robespierre *(1758-1794)*

against the more radical and sans-culotte "terrorists" and there were soon new trials and purges.

In the autumn of 1794, the General Maximum was abandoned, allowing food prices to rise. A very harsh winter followed, with widespread shortage and real starvation.

1795

In the spring of 1795, sans-culotte forces in Paris tried to rise against the Convention, demanding material aid and the enacting of the 1793 democratic constitution. They managed to seize control of the chamber for a few hours before being crushed, their actions adding to demands for rigorous repression of "terrorist" groups.

The military situation had been turned around: from successful national defence in 1794, France went on in 1795 to occupy the Netherlands, secure favourable peace terms from Prussia and Spain (turning the latter into an ally the next year), and in 1796 attacked Austrian power in Italy. Overseas colonies had fallen to Britain, with its strong navy, but within Europe there was now the potential for French military domination.

In late August 1795 the Convention published the "Constitution of the Year III", introducing annual elections, a bicameral legislature and a five-man collective "head of state" – the Directory. The "Law of Two-Thirds" required that two-thirds of those who first took national office in the new legislature were members of the old Convention. A structural balancing act was accompanied by a political one: potentially radical clubs and popular societies were banned, and when in October royalists launched violent protests in Paris, they were crushed and further repressive laws introduced.

1796-7

Throughout 1796, as General Bonaparte's army rampaged through northern Italy, the Directory tried to rule in a centrist manner, still facing violent threats from both radicals and royalists. Peace with Austria in 1797 left France dominant in northern and central Italy, and turning its attention to the possibility of an invasion of Britain.

Elections in the spring of 1797 saw the old Convention members ousted en masse from the legislature, with a strong swing to the right amongst electors. The political crisis this threatened was met in September with a purge led by the Directory and the army, and an apparent swing to the left in national policy. But when in the spring of 1798 the electorate responded by choosing more radical candidates, they too were purged, as an "extreme centre" of republican leadership treated their control over the state as more important than voters' wishes.

> *The French economy was suffering from rampant inflation. Paper money printing and the loot of military campaigns were the state's only resources. Tax-collection and many other aspects of civil existence were non-functional, as echoes of the Terror continued to drive factional conflict at the local level.*

1798-9

Military expansionism reached a peak in the summer of 1798. Bonaparte's expedition to Egypt first seized Malta, then smashed Turkish power along the Nile. At the same time there was a short-lived but real possibility of a French army linking up with insurrection in Ireland. However, British naval victory at Aboukir Bay in August cut Bonaparte off from reinforcement, and at the end of the year the Kingdom of Naples joined Britain and Russia against France, threatening the Republic's Italian position.

In the spring of 1799, French aggression pushed Austria into the enemy alliance. Allied forces, accompanied by popular pro-Catholic risings, drove the French out of almost all their Italian territories.

Internally, elections were closely monitored, but still produced a legislature at odds with the Directory, while in the summer open royalist insurrections broke out. The Directory itself was forcibly purged under pressure from the legislature in June, and an atmosphere of pervasive crisis endured thereafter.

General Bonaparte, abandoning his army in Egypt, reached France in October, and became the figurehead of an existing group of authoritarian centrist conspirators; in less than a month the conspiracy acted, and in a *coup d'état* the Directorial constitution was overthrown in favour of a "Consulate" – a supposedly collective form of government that Bonaparte rapidly came to dominate.

Why has the French Revolution caused so much argument?

There has never been, and probably never will be, agreement on how to understand the French Revolution. It divided not only France, but all of Europe, as soon as it began. In Britain it was first greeted as France "catching up" with the kind of parliamentary institutions they had had in place for a century, but within a year a much more divisive debate opened up.

Edmund Burke, an MP and prominent member of the Whig party, who had supported American independence, saw in France something infinitely more dangerous. His *Reflections on the Revolution in France* (1790) painted a picture of a society tearing itself apart from within, as ignorant mobs and abstract political speculators formed an unholy alliance to destroy time-honoured social structures.

His former friend Thomas Paine, who had been an even more active supporter of the American cause, answered him the following year with the *Rights of Man*, a blistering attack on the idea that past generations could dictate political arrangements to the future. He called for Britons to join the Franco-American tide of change. Their debate split society. Working men formed

"Corresponding Societies" to debate reform. The response was a decade of intensifying repression – to the extent that Britain might be said to have experienced all the evils of a counter-revolution without ever having a revolution.

While the French example was causing havoc in Britain, observers across Europe were debating the causes of the strife. Accustomed to seeing "great men" as the driving force of politics in an aristocratic society, many insisted that there had to be a leading will behind the Revolution. The abbé Barruel produced a *History of Jacobinism* in 1797 which treated the events of the 1790s as the outcome of a conspiracy of anti-Catholic forces: the leading thinkers of the Enlightenment, Freemasonry and the (largely imaginary) Illuminati all forming the foundations of the "Jacobin" spirit of the radical revolutionaries.

The notion of leaders with hidden motivations allied to a corruptible mob echoed down the following century – in Charles Dickens's *Tale of Two Cities*, for example, and in the work of the French historian Hippolyte Taine, who gave immensely detailed (and largely false) accounts of the way popular violence had been whipped up by corrupting gold.

The European left had learned very different lessons from the Revolution. Starting with a generation of radical liberal historians in the 1820s and 30s, it was interpreted as a structural change in society that allowed the capitalist "bourgeoisie" to achieve a political freedom to match its economic power. More socially radical historians also promoted the notion that "the people" had shown their distinctive spirit in the 1790s, in rising up to defend their rights, and the nation's freedom.

These ideas came together as part of the foundations of socialist political thought. Karl Marx explicitly developed the idea that revolutionary change was a necessary part of historical development. As Marxism, and later Communism, became globally powerful ideologies in the early to mid-20th centuries, the idea that the French Revolution was a significant stage in social evolution became dominant in Western understandings of it.

The fall of Communism from 1989, and the rise of more self-consciously anti-communist thought in the West which had already marked the 1970s and 1980s, shifted the historical field. Without quite reaching back to the conspiracy-mongering of Barruel, the French historian François Furet in the 1970s pinned the revolutionary trauma on "societies of thought" – educated men with agendas. For Furet, the central experience and lesson of the Revolution was of the dangerous power of ideology to run amok, creating its own "reality" in which the actual rights and lives of individuals were devalued.

While such authors put forward essentially academic arguments against the prevailing consensus of the Revolution as a historical necessity, Simon Schama produced *Citizens*, a best-selling narrative for a wider audience that held up the Terror as something truly terrible, and as the outcome of a Revolution inflicted on a society that had been flourishing. It was driven by forces that, in his version, looked and sounded very much like the villains Edmund Burke had promoted 200 years earlier: bloodthirsty mobs and callous, manipulative leaders.[2]

Schama's work is a particularly vivid illustration of the fact that histories of the French Revolution are all written in political contexts, and carry political messages: in his case, that revolutionary change is always a bad thing, led by bad people. Few recent academic interpretations have been that bald, although they continue to cover a wide political spectrum.

In many respects, the more we have unearthed about the detailed history of events from 1789 and after, the more scope has been created for people to draw their own conclusions about which aspects of the evolving situation were the really important ones, and why. We now have to hand, for example, intimate records of the life of the royal family, and equally intimate accounts of the hopes and fears of groups and individuals everywhere from the aristocracy and mercantile classes to the sans-culottes of Paris and the provincial peasantry. Archival records have been mined to show us how every section of society thought – and, not least, have drawn attention to the haze of fear and confusion that hung over everything they did. Every succeeding generation has had to make up their own minds about the French Revolution. There is no sign of that ceasing to be true any time soon.

Pre-Revolution

What caused the French Revolution?

The debate between radical and conservative views of revolution is often a debate about structures and intentions. Was collapse built into the evils of a cruelly hierarchical society, or was a functioning and developing society plunged into chaos by opportunists exploiting a temporary setback? In that sense, the debate has classically been one between *social* and *political* interpretations, although it is also one about long and short term causes, and, more recently, about how much cultural issues need to be considered.

Within the sphere of the social, the key question since the 1820s has been the rise of the middle class. Since this class, and its attendant capitalist values, clearly triumphed in the 19th century, it was generally taken for granted by scholars that it had played a decisive role in events. Revisionist studies in the 1960s and 1970s, however, queried this, showing that the link between the kind of people who took leading roles in the Revolution and any kind of "capitalist" values was weak. Career paths, even for merchants, tended to end with buying land and titles and aspiring to become noble. Colin Lucas famously called the bourgeoisie in this system a "transitional category of indeterminate social mutants", with no clear collective difference in goals from the established elite.[3]

But while a simple link between class structure, economic change and revolution was broken by the work of Lucas, among others, more recent scholarship has shown that capitalist values were without doubt intruding more and more into French society. Colin Jones argues that a flourishing provincial press in the late 18th century promoted a consumer culture, disseminating commercial information and providing a marketplace for all kinds of transactions. Lauren Clay documents an ardently pro-capitalist culture amongst regional and nationwide networks of merchants, while also showing how the swelling trade with Caribbean slave colonies was transforming the economy.[4]

One important way of understanding these apparent contradictions comes through Timothy

Tackett's work on the individuals who would become revolutionary politicians. While many of the bourgeois people displayed the ambiguities just discussed, what emerged very clearly by the time of the Revolution was that most of the nobles involved remained absolutely certain that they were a separate order – indeed, for some, a separate race. Thus if in quieter times this group could cope with a blending at the edges from "social mutants", they remained committed to a difference that, in revolutionary crisis, became a decisive rupture.[5]

How did the changing political culture breed revolution?

One reason this rupture would prove so traumatic is that the language of politics had for decades been drifting towards a denial of the hierarchical divisions of society. Throughout the 18th century, a long series of disputes had played out between the royal government and the *parlements* – regional law-courts that, because of their role in registering new laws and taxes, and their numerous aristocratic membership, viewed themselves as guardians of the constitution. *Parlementaire* judges, as they disputed the boundaries of royal power, shaped a language of the "Nation" as a body with an identity that could not simply be subsumed within the passive loyalty of subjects to a monarch.

As this was happening, the more general developments of the Enlightenment brought two political ideas into focus: the first was that public dissemination of information was good in itself, contributing to the formation of a "public" as an informed and rational body. The second, following from this, was a growing view that such a public formed by its existence a "public opinion" that was effectively a rational consensus. Remarkably, despite remaining deeply concerned about actual circulation of information, and running an intensive censorship apparatus down to 1789, even the government came to accept from the later 1770s that this "public opinion" existed, as did a "national" interest.

A significant dimension of the increasingly overt political debate of Louis XVI's reign was the contest between ministers and *parlementaires* – and the journalists, pamphleteers and other authors on both sides – about which of them better represented "public opinion". This language would soon come into shattering collision with both the royal state, and the underlying noble conviction of superiority.

Why was France in such bad shape?

Revolution arrived when it did not for any compelling structural reason but out of the state's inability to change. In some senses this is true of all the great historical revolutions of the West – Charles I and Nicholas II blundered their way into collision with their populations, as in a slightly different way did George III's ministers over the Thirteen Colonies. The French case was a particularly elaborate failure, however, and one for which Louis XVI cannot be held wholly responsible.

It is an abiding irony that enthusiastic French support for American independence, resulting in five years of overt warfare after several years of more covert action, broke the back of the French fiscal system. When royal minister and acclaimed financial genius Jacques Necker took out huge loans to finance the fighting from 1778, he was tacitly admitting the inability of the taxation system to deliver the necessary resources, while also piling a significant new burden of repayment on a structure that had groaned for decades to repay the debts occurred in earlier wars.

Royal ministers had long recognised this problem: the later 1760s were full of reform plans, but *parlementaire* opposition had been so effective that Louis XV had been forced to dissolve the *parlements* in 1771 to try to get movement. In a further irony, this dissolution made the king so unpopular that Louis XVI, coming to the throne three years later, felt he had no choice but to reverse it. But then the extensive reform plans of his own minister, Anne Robert Jacques Turgot, were blocked in 1776 by conservative forces across the institutions of the state, including the restored *parlements*, leaving no clear route to funding the American War except the one Necker took.

The underlying problem was twofold: firstly, the taxation system itself was impossibly complex. It was much better at taking money from poor peasants than wealthy noblemen, and cemented into the culture of privilege that marked out hierarchical social status. To be important was to be exempt from the major burdens of taxation. Thus to threaten to make taxation more effective was to threaten a foundation of the elite's self-definition.

Secondly, the baroque complexity of tax-collecting arrangements, and their extensive opportunities for private profit, made it very easy to blame fiscal under-performance not on privilege, but on corruption. This turned the spotlight of accusation on the very royal ministers who were increasingly desperate to achieve reform.

This was particularly clear in the case of Charles Alexandre de Calonne, finance minister from November 1783. Using major programmes of public spending to boost confidence in the state, while wrestling behind the scenes with the facts of a debt mountain rapidly approaching the point of unsustainability, he was extremely vulnerable to charges of both personal profligacy and structural corruption when, from late 1786, he began to attempt reform.

What were the main obstacles to reform?

Calonne could not have known that his reform plans were probably doomed by the very act of calling the Assembly of Notables, but the men drawn together in February 1787 proved to have a combination of views fundamentally opposed to the vision of reform the government was offering.

On the one hand, the plans to reduce and remove privileged exemptions from taxation, and to give the privileged class no special access to planned new administrative assemblies, were attacked as an assault on the privileged class itself. On the other, the half-hearted gestures towards permanent consultative bodies were condemned as a thin cover for despotism, with a new sense of national identity requiring a permanent Estates-General.

Calonne's failure to persuade his opponents, especially after making the argument public with a denunciatory text he distributed to be read in every pulpit nationwide, brought him down in April. But his replacement, Loménie de Brienne, offered nothing new. Unable to gain traction with the

Notables, Brienne dissolved the Assembly and tried to force measures through the *parlements* in the summer of 1787. This just consolidated the deadlock.

For the next year, political argument returned to its habitual course. Ministers assailed the *parlements* with demands to approve reform, and the judges refused, increasingly presenting the idea of the Estates-General as the only legitimate way to make such major changes. A partial compromise was reached in the autumn of 1787: some reforms were withdrawn in return for the acceptance of some new taxes and loans, and the king agreed that the Estates-General would have to meet eventually (before 1792). But this was soured in November when the king also demanded enforced registration of these plans without permitting the judges to debate them. Vehement protests followed. Given that the king was still a firm believer in the absolute nature of his own powers, only an escalation of the crisis could break the deadlock.

This came in the spring of 1788, when the *parlements* were abolished. There was riotous resistance – most famously in Grenoble's "Day of Tiles" – as armed force was used to arrest judges and close down their institutions. The events of the previous year had been watched and commented on with feverish intensity by the public and there was general uproar at the crown's move. The result was a further collapse in the state's credit, and, by the late summer, looming bankruptcy.

Brienne had to suspend his changes to the *parlements* and agree to call the Estates-General for the spring of 1789. In late August he was forced from office, discredited by court intrigue. Necker was recalled in his place, and by the end of August, had cancelled all the recent reforms and restored the *parlements* to their full powers, awaiting the Estates-General.

On 25 September, the restored judges of the Paris *parlement* declared that the only proper way for the Estates-General to meet was to follow the "forms of 1614" – its last actual session. The Catholic clergy, the nobility, and the rest of the population would form three separate "Estates", each debating and voting in its own chamber. The privileged

THE MIND OF THE KING

Louis XVI came to the throne while still (just) a teenager, repulsed by the debauchery of his predecessor, still working out an awkward marital life with his young wife Marie Antoinette, but committed to Enlightenment principles. By the end of the 1770s, he was a loving father, maturing into his role, leading a successful war against the old British enemy, but also already showing signs of the chronic indecision, and tendency to follow the advice of those who spoke last, that would dog his later life.

Louis's basic problem, as the "pre-Revolution" loomed, was that he was a modern man, preferring a very "bourgeois" domesticity to the baroque pomp of the

classes would have an inbuilt majority over the representatives of the great mass of the population.

What had appeared as a triumph for "national" opposition to royal despotism was suddenly exposed as a power grab by the privileged minority, causing an eruption of dissent from Third Estate writers. The Paris *parlement* reacted with censorship, destroying its public reputation. Necker's efforts to resolve this new crisis with a Second Assembly of Notables just revealed deeply entrenched resistance to equality amongst the privileged.

At the end of the year a royal decree authorised the election of twice as many Third Estate deputies as for each of the other two orders and lifted press censorship on discussing the electoral process. It failed, however, to say whether this doubled

---

Court or energetic political strife – but he also remained convinced that he did rule by divine right, and that nobody could or should take that from him. His political programme remained remarkably consistent through to 1789 – what his ministers had sought from the Assembly of Notables, an easing of fiscal privileges and a renewed and rationalised administration, was what he offered the National Assembly on 23 June.

Everything he conceded after that, from the abolition of privilege and Declaration of Rights onwards, was an unwilling gesture.

There were a few signs in 1790 that he was trying to compromise on a day-to-day basis, but the queen's correspondence makes it clear that by the end of that year the royal couple were plotting both escape and a return to the 23 June programme. Marie Antoinette was the more

representation would be counted "by head" when actual votes were taken. France entered 1789 with what had been a fight between the monarch and the nation suddenly transformed into one about the nature of that nation itself.

Why was the hierarchical society of the Old Regime so hard to change?

To a modern reader, the French "Pre-Revolution" of 1787-88 can seem inexplicable, as leading figures make arguments for liberty with one side of their mouth, while demanding privilege with the other. A frequent historiographical response has been to dismiss all this as hypocritical manoeuvring, and skip on to the events of 1789. But the way in which the monarchical state collapsed does show us important features about

forceful personality of the royal couple, something for which she suffered grotesque demonisation at the hands of radical journalists and officials. Louis was increasingly passive, which some see as an acceptance of Christian martyrdom – the damage done to the Catholic church loomed large in his papers. Others believe he suffered from depression from the end of 1789 onwards.

There is no doubt that, especially after the failed attempt to flee in June 1791, Louis saw himself as a helpless prisoner. When he took the oath to the new Constitution that autumn he was committing perjury in that he never intended to honour it, but he was driven

it, and about the conflicts to come.

These years are at the exact threshold between a pre-modern social landscape that takes hierarchical difference for granted as a fact of (God-given) nature, and a modern world of nations and classes that values either identity or conflict in explaining social structure.[6] The work of John Hardman and Vivian Gruder has shown that all the individuals and factions involved appear to have believed very firmly in their right to make the arguments they did, even when those arguments were also, blatantly, moves in a game of power.

The society that the *parlements* and the Notables were seeking to protect from royal despotism was one in which oppression had been normalised. It was the logical underpinning of the networks of privilege that ran through every level of the hierarchy. The wealthier and more powerful you were, the more distanced you were from any real obligation to attend to anything except your own

to the humiliating submission in the hope of saving his children's lives. He wept openly as soon as he escaped the public gaze of the ceremony. The desperate and self-destructive decision to gamble on support for a war, in the hope of French defeat, followed from all of this, as did his surrender on 10th August 1792, before a shot had been fired.

By the time of his fall, let alone his trial and execution on 21st January, 1793, his own emigrated brothers, and many of the leaders of the counter-revolution, had already given up on Louis as anything other than a useful martyr to their cause. ■

interests. Your right not to be taxed as ordinary people were was as much part of your identity as your name.

At lower social levels, such patterns were replicated. Different provinces held different historical entitlements to avoid taxes or services imposed on others, and these formed their core identity. Towns held privileges that distinguished them from the relatively unprivileged peasants outside their walls, and, within those walls, different groups of office holders and craft guilds held their own privileges. It would be difficult to find anyone except a homeless beggar who could not claim some kind of local privilege, but for most these privileges were a pale shadow of those enjoyed by the powerful, holding them barely above an abyss of marginalisation. In that sense, the privileges of many merely confirmed their position close to the bottom of a steep hierarchy

Beyond the historically-grounded dissemination of privileges against state taxation, there was also a wider array of privileges grounded in ideas of social difference. Just as noble status purportedly made you a different kind of person in relation to the state, so "feudal" privileges and rights – historically associated with noble status – could put you not just above, but over, others. To be a *seigneur*, a "lord of the manor", entitled you to a share of harvests, annual fees, tolls, and monopoly charges for mills and other services, covering anything from a part of a village to a whole county-sized area. You need not own any of the actual land involved: as long as you owned the feudal rights over it, the inhabitants and cultivators owed you a significant chunk of their income.

So taken-for-granted was this structure, that over the 18th century land ownership had increasingly become an investment of choice for middle-class individuals aspiring to security and leisure as their careers developed. These buyers expected a healthy return on their investment, and had no hesitation in employing ruthless agents, bailiffs and lawyers to get it – aided by the fact that seigneurial status often gave you the right to hold local courts in your own name, judging those who owed you money. The hierarchy of privilege was not just a passive environment, but was an active, often aggressive, force holding down ordinary people.

How did the political culture enforce the social structure?

The sense of a repressive hierarchy also dominated the political and cultural realms. Royal disputes with the *parlements* hinged on notions of absolutism which invested the monarch with the power to act as he saw fit in making laws and conducting policy. Where the *parlements* objected to this model of royal power, it was often because they sought to tie that power more firmly to respect for elite privileges instead. Both sides might increasingly use a language of public opinion and national interest, but until the breakdown of 1788 such rhetoric overlay a consensus to keep most of the population firmly subjugated.

The general approach to information enforced this consensus. Both the royal state and the Catholic Church assumed a right to control what people read, saw and thought. Censorship was seen as a natural state of affairs, guiding and shaping a healthy public debate by weeding out all that was disruptive and potentially corrupting. Royal censors took an active role in discussing with authors how their works could be made more acceptable in this system, and their statements of approval were printed in the final product. Both the Church and the courts took dramatic action, including the burning of books and imprisonment of authors, when this system was breached. Active control over information continued, and in some cases became more effective, right down to the eve of the Revolution, despite all that was said about "public opinion" and its value.

Control over individuals followed a similar pattern. In its harshest form it was marked by the use of *lettres de cachet* ("letters under seal") which gave royal authority for the detention without trial of a named person. Very widely used to detain those suffering mental health problems, such orders

Madame du Barry, the the old king Louis XV's scandalous mistress, painted by François-Hubert Drouais

were also granted to families seeking to control rebellious teenage (or older) children. In addition, they had a notorious existence as a system for ensuring that any dangerous or disruptive individual could be confined, sent to a convent, exiled, stripped of office or otherwise dealt with, without a public hearing or right of appeal. Royal authorities were rumoured to be extremely obliging in the granting of such orders to superiors in a wide range of contexts, from army regiments to religious institutions, casting a shadow of fear over any resistance to abuse of power.

Systems of censorship and control were the responsibility of what was known as the *police*, the umbrella term for the different authorities which kept society in order. In Paris, for example street-sweeping, street lighting, market hours, weights and measures, and wet-nursing all came under supervision of *la police*. So, throughout France, did the secret practice of spying on the population for potential dissent, and the seizing and interrogating of suspected dissenters. In their wider, administrative role, the *police* covered a great deal of economic life, so that apprentice tradesmen and women, and those who had passed their apprenticeship to work as regular employees, were subject to the authority of guild masters controlling who they could work for, where they worked, and what they were authorised to make and sell. When guilds tried to police the boundaries of their jurisdictions, raiding workshops where "unlicensed" work was taking place and dragging competitors through the courts, they showed the many different spheres in which the whole "Old Regime" rejected the very idea of general freedom.

In Paris in particular, where the population of some 700,000 was seen as a continuous threat to good order, dozens (and rumoured hundreds) of police spies moved through the public spaces and the taverns. Often themselves former criminals, their existence was well known, despised and feared. When the Revolution came, the evils of this system would soon be loudly denounced, even though, ironically, revolutionary authorities never stopped paying men to watch the population and report on its words.

How effective was the censorship on which the "system" depended?

The way in which all these systems operated before 1789 was freighted with heavy ironies, some of which contributed to the Revolution itself. The decades before 1789 are the period of the Enlightenment, when radical new forms of knowledge and debate spread through the literate classes, raising, among other things, the spectre of "public opinion" that penetrated to the heart of pre-revolutionary politics. This happened because royal authorities, and the social elite in general, never actually treated the system of secrecy and censorship as if it applied to them.

The aristocratic Parisian dinner-parties that history knows as the *salons* were one arena in which the elite played with new ideas. Hostesses cultivated tastes for new literature, plays and poetry and encouraged discussion of everything from science and mathematics to Court gossip and popular rumour. The membership of the *salons* was dominated by the wealthy and noble elite, but other authors and observers from the lower ranks were also admitted under the protection of patrons. The *salon* environment prided itself on its free-flowing discussion and relative equality, and has often been taken by historians at its own valuation, but Antoine Lilti has recently brought to light the extent to which it fundamentally relied on an aristocratic and hierarchical context to function.[7]

It was in this context that the strange relationship between state censorship and the wider world of publishing played out. Right from the start of the 18th century, elite reformers had sought to reach an elite "public" with their works, and found themselves at odds with censors. From the 1750s, as the *salon* culture firmly embedded itself, royal ministers in charge of the book trade began quietly allowing more "dangerous" publications, sharing the general enlightened view that discussion of reform would be healthy for the kingdom. Such tacit permission was confined to works that circulated at a price that kept them out of the hands of common people. It was not a free-for-all, but it nonetheless reinforced the sense that the law did not apply to important people.

Alongside this, royal authorities wrestled with a swelling illegal book trade. Extensively documented by the historians Robert Darnton and Simon Burrows, the capacity of printers and publishers to operate in territories outside French control, and smuggle their wares into the country, meant that throughout the pre-revolutionary decades almost anyone in the middling and upper classes had access to reading matter that it was a crime to possess. Much of this was frankly obscene, as a pornographic approach was used by authors to lampoon the Church, royal ministers and Court factions.

Until recently, it was thought that this tide swelled to a flood in the 1780s and embraced explicit (in every sense) condemnations of Louis XVI and Marie Antoinette. Work by Burrows and Louise Seaward has challenged this, suggesting that the crown fought hard, and much of the time successfully, to keep such material out of circulation. But to do so they often had to pay large sums to blackmailing authors, and lock up the offending texts, literally, in the Bastille.[8]

There were deep and paradoxical ambiguities in this cultural landscape. In the mid-1780s, Louis XVI was successfully persuaded by Marie Antoinette and other members of his family to allow the production of the play *The Marriage of Figaro*, a sex-comedy in which aristocratic morals were condemned amongst much bed-hopping innuendo. The king thought it highly dangerous, but the rest of the Court merely found it hilarious, as did the wider Parisian audiences when it went on a record-breaking run of performances. Aristocratic audiences seemed not to have noticed the social critique that later generations identified as a starting point of the Revolution. But that hindsight itself may be misplaced, for serious-minded critics at the time did not applaud the "subversive" message of the play, seeing it instead as a symptom of aristocratic decadence, manifesting perverse morals and encouraging adultery.

In the realm of culture, France by the 1780s was in a place of confusion. Through the illegal book trade, everything from obscene histories of Louis XV's mistresses to denunciations of the *lettres de cachet* was in wide circulation. Through the privileges of the *parlements*, lawyers could write openly and legally about court cases that cast the elite in a bad light, composing stories of abuse of power that sold

ROUSSEAU'S LEGACY

The philosopher Jean-Jacques Rousseau (1712-1778) had an extraordinary influence on the French Revolution. The exact nature of that influence, however, has puzzled historians for generations. In his 1762 work *On the Social Contract*, Rousseau appeared to give a blueprint for a republican constitution animated by a democratic "General Will" of the people. Counter-revolutionary writers quickly settled on this as one of the sources of revolutionary evil.

Historical reality appears rather more complex. Rousseau's General Will is hard to distinguish on the page from other ideas about public opinion circulating in the period; he imagines it emerging not through debate, but through silent contemplation by each citizen. Rousseau also stands out against elected assemblies and representation, declaring them unfit means to govern a great country.

There is also debate about how widely the *Social Contract* was actually read. Almost every revolutionary

by the thousand. In the attics and taverns of Paris, new generations of young writers were trying to scrape a living under police surveillance.

Over it all, the abiding doctrine that the state could, would and must control, censor and condemn dissent continued to reign, but even the minister Calonne used the press to enter into a scathing public dispute with the Assembly of Notables. A sense that the system was unbreakable seemed to coexist with very firm efforts, at every level, to break it.

---

had certainly "read Rousseau", but he was more often invoked as a touchstone for his "sublime" belief in virtue than for any particular structural insight. Through his writings on education (*Emile*), his sentimental epistolary novel *Julie, or the New Héloïse*, and his searingly frank autobiography, the *Confessions*, Rousseau created an ideal of behaviour that was at once deeply personal – oriented around authentic emotional experiences – and yet also political. The "Rousseauist" individual cherished genuine feeling, particularly sympathy for suffering, and was thus marked out against the cold cynicism of the stereotypical aristocrat. Once other circumstances had created space for it to flourish, this world view became central to the "Jacobin" identity.

Robespierre was a passionate devotee of Rousseau – but so too were many of his Girondin enemies. Ironically, Rousseau the man was by his own account deeply unpleasant – abandoning his own children to a foundling hospital, he routinely abused the generosity of a series of wealthy hosts, and entered into paranoid feuds with almost every figure of repute he came across. ■

Revolution

How did men and women of the old order become revolutionaries?

To add to the general confusion of the era, we must recognise that the complex and ultimately unsuccessful efforts to save the Old Regime from collapse through the 1770s and 1780s included many genuine, enlightened reforms. P.M. Jones has extensively documented the real debates amongst government officials, and the pioneering changes they succeeded in introducing. Necker's ministry during the American War set up two trial Provincial Assemblies in Berry and Haute-Guienne which functioned thereafter on a representative basis down to the Revolution. Their 48 members were co-opted rather than elected, but saw rural and urban non-noble elites sitting on an equal footing with nobles and clergy, empowered to apportion local taxes and pursue projects of public works and agricultural reform.[9]

Calonne's unsuccessful relationship with the Assembly of Notables in 1787 masks a further successful step towards representative institutions. He brought around 20 new Provincial Assemblies into existence in that year. Their membership was, again, co-opted from elites, but at a lower level of Municipal Assemblies representation was thrown open to election, and tens of thousands of propertied voters went to the polls in an active political process in 1787. Without conceding any royal power in practice, the government was nonetheless opening up the question of how social structure and political institutions should be related. Observers at the time, including Americans, thought France was progressing towards a new, balanced, constitution.

America – its independence, and the constitutional arrangements of the new United States – provided another strong stimulus to thoughts of change. The war fought there may have had dire fiscal consequences for the French state, but the French elite widely embraced what they understood to be the pure and natural virtues of the new nation. A significant cohort of noble officers fought with the French expeditionary force, or, like the Marquis de Lafayette, were so keen that they volunteered to serve in the American army itself. While some of the enthusiasm may have come from the chance to humiliate the British victors of 1763, many even of the most distinguished noblemen seem genuinely to have admired the American spirit, and been fascinated by the process of constituting the new states.

Lafayette was a member of the Assembly of Notables, and voiced his principles there by asking when France could expect a "truly national representation" to be created. He also kept a framed copy of the US Declaration of Independence in his home, with an empty frame beside it for a French declaration of rights. As the crisis of the Pre-revolution developed, such elite commitment to change expanded. From November 1788 the so-called "Society of Thirty" began to meet regularly in the capital to promote the Estates-General. Actually numbering more than 50, this group included noblemen, judges and senior clerics. Around half the membership came from the highest echelons of the military and Court nobility.

The language of such men, and that of the far wider reading classes of France, had come to accept almost without question that "public opinion" and the rights of the Third Estate should come to the fore in new structures – though, as their enemies soon charged, the members of the Society of Thirty also expected that their distinguished origins and principles would give them a right to a leading role in a new polity. This was just one more layer of contradiction, soon to be cut through by direct political conflict.

How did French society respond to the calling of the Estates-General?

From the end of 1788, Necker's ministry took a remarkably hands-off approach to the Estates-

General, perhaps influenced by the belief that public opinion would see reason. Traditional worries about public order in Paris caused elections there to be delayed and tightly controlled, but elsewhere they went ahead on an extraordinarily broad basis, and with the traditional royal summons for subjects to make their grievances known. The lack of governmental management, and the surrounding public debate, led to two major developments.

Firstly, the fault-line of privilege opened up by the Paris parlement continued to widen. Famously, the abbé Sieyès, an intellectual cleric and member of the Society of Thirty, published *What is the Third Estate?* in January 1789. This was a book-length polemical pamphlet summed up in its most famous lines:

> What is the Third Estate? Everything. What has it been hitherto in the political order? Nothing. What does it desire to be? Something.

In making this argument, Sieyes also lambasted the privileged orders as parasites on the body politic – an intriguing argument from a man who moved in Parisian high society.

It was not in Paris, but rather in the provinces, that Sieyès's attack, and others like it, struck home. Timothy Tackett has shown that these months saw a rallying to the defence of noble identities from the tens of thousands of provincial noblemen, often army officers, whose voices had not been heard in the pre-revolution. They had little doubt that their social existence was threatened. They frequently took the circulation of political information from groups such as the Society of Thirty as evidence of a conspiracy against them.

Such circulation was part of the second major development: the emergence of the *cahiers de doléances*, a landmark moment in history. These "registers of grievance" were the traditional accompaniment to the Estates-General, intended to form its agenda for redress. Under the conditions of long-running crisis and mass

FALLEN IDOLS NO.1
THE MARQUIS
DE LAFAYETTE
(1757-1834)

Marie Joseph Paul Yves Roch Gilbert du Motier de Lafayette was the "Hero of Two Worlds", who as a young nobleman had defied authority to join George Washington in the army of the American rebels, and rose to become a general. He plotted with Thomas Jefferson, US ambassador in Paris, to give France a Declaration of Rights even before the Estates-General met.

His vision, however, was limited to political rather than social reform, and when in the summer of 1789 he took on a role as commander of the Parisian National Guard, he soon found himself fighting daily battles against plebeian demands for change.

participation of early 1789, they became something remarkable. No brief summary can do justice to the volume of words that poured forth from every village, neighbourhood, and craft guild.

Some texts took an expansive view of the structural problems of the French state, some concentrated on personal liberties or economic development, many lamented the local suffering and injustices stemming from nationwide structures of privilege and oppression. These were amalgamated into more than 600 *cahiers* to be carried by representatives, alongside those drafted by meetings of nobles and clergy. The historian Alexis de Tocqueville made a pioneering study of

---

His popularity was at its height during the Festival of Federation in July 1790, but as his reputation as a fierce authoritarian solidified, he developed a vendetta against the Jacobin movement, many of whom saw him as little better than a counter-revolutionary.

He failed catastrophically to be elected Mayor of Paris in late 1791, and took command of a front line army as war loomed. Lafayette returned to Paris in June 1792 with a half-formed plan for a coup d'état against the Jacobin-led Legislative Assembly. Betrayed by Marie Antoinette, who hated him for bringing the royal couple to Paris in the October Days, and under threat of impeachment for abandoning his post, he returned to the front. He tried to lead his army on the capital after the fall of the monarchy but, when the troops refused to march, instead defected to the Austrians. Despite this act of treachery, he lived long enough to become a totem of liberal values in the Revolution of 1830. ■

them in the mid-19th century, and his judgement has never been bettered:

> I have read attentively the *cahiers* of the Three Estates ... I observe that here a law and there a custom is sought to be changed, and I note it. Pursuing the immense task to the end, and adding together all the separate demands, I discover with terror that nothing less is demanded than the simultaneous and systematic repeal of all the laws and the abolition of all the customs prevailing in the country; and I perceive at once that one of the great revolutions the world ever saw is impending.[10]

Estates-General representatives, or "deputies", gathered at Versailles at the start of May 1789 with all the nervous energy of the *cahiers* and the divisive public debate behind them. As with the elections, the government failed to control the situation by setting a clear agenda, not even ensuring that the first stage of the body's formation – the verification of individual deputies' credentials – went ahead speedily.

The loudest voices in the Third Estate demanded that the three Estates meet as one; the loudest voices in the nobility and clergy refused. Stalemate ensued. Timothy Tackett's work, again, has shown how the outcome of this was a dynamic radicalisation on both sides, with the Third Estate talking themselves into dramatic declarations of their identity as a National Assembly, and making an oath on 20th June to write a new constitution, while nobles (outside the elite grouping that had emerged from the Society of Thirty) saw this as the fomentation of revolt, and dug in to resist.

Royal failure to give a positive lead swung in late June to an attempt to dictate a reform package which had already been surpassed by Third Estate demands. In early July the crown plotted a coup to replace Necker with a government that would crack down hard on dissent. Many of the Third Estate deputies were terrified for their lives. It was at this stage that the parallel revolution amongst the common people came to the fore.

How significant were the popular uprisings of 1789?

The pre-revolution of 1787-8 had already seen episodes of dramatic popular involvement: demonstrations in Paris in favour of the beleaguered *parlement* in 1787, protests and riots in regional centres when the *parlements* were closed down in 1788, and protests about food prices and shortages in the same year. The 1788 harvest was terribly small, and the subsequent winter very harsh, adding to a steep economic downturn caused by political uncertainty and an ill-judged free trade treaty with Britain. Thus the elections for the Estates-General had been held in a nationwide atmosphere of not merely political but material crisis.

Across the country, the outcome of the drafting of the *cahiers de doléances* was a realisation, particularly by rural communities, that they did not have passively to accept the oppressive structures they lived under. Observers from the upper classes glossed this as a naive peasant belief that by stating their problems they had ended them, obtaining royal permission not to pay taxes, tithes or feudal dues. But in practice their scorn was soon turned to alarm by very real resistance to such payments, and by news of communities going even further.

By the spring of 1789, reports were coming from around France of tax offices being pillaged and their records burned, of wealthy abbeys forced to open their storehouses, and of the slaughter of rabbits, deer and fowl in aristocrats' private game reserves. In many areas, villagers marched to confront their local feudal lords, breaking down fences enclosing pastureland, demanding the return of crops surrendered in tithes and dues after the last harvest, and seeking out and destroying the charters and registers that recorded their obligations as vassals.

Lords and their agents, tax officials, bishops and other elite witnesses were paralysed by horror at this insurrection, which they alternated between seeing as madness or the outcome of some shadowy conspiracy. Historical analysis, however, demonstrates that popular actions were nearly always relatively restrained, and targeted at specific abuses. Wanton destruction and killing was almost absent, and violence against persons in general was limited, especially given the months of activity and the hundreds of thousands involved.

Major rioting reached Paris in late April 1789, when two factory owners were rumoured to have called for wage cuts. Amidst spiralling food prices, the popular reaction was the gutting of both men's houses, along with the factory of the one, Réveillon, who gives his name to the episode. The state's response to this defiance was an assault by the military garrison that killed at least several dozen. In a marker of the cultural barriers between popular action and elite perspectives, even the American ambassador, Thomas Jefferson, an ardent supporter of reform, wrote of the riots as the "unprovoked and unpitied" folly of "the most abandoned banditti".[11]

Only ten weeks later, the deputies of the National Assembly would burst into almost hysterical tears of relief when they came to understand that the insurrection of Paris between 12th and 14th July was directed in their defence, and not some fiendish part of an aristocratic plan for their destruction. The events that culminated in the storming of the Bastille demonstrated a remarkable, near-unanimous mobilisation by the capital against the feared aristocrats and their grip on the state. The hundred people who perished under cannon fire on the 14th were mostly artisans and workers, and the middle class leaders who took charge of the city – emerging from the electoral assemblies that had met in the spring here – soon had a force of more than 60,000 under arms from every social class.

Popular action transformed the French Revolution into something larger than a merely political crisis, and popular action saved the national "patriot" leadership from being snuffed out by the crown in July 1789. But elite attitudes did not change overnight. The Parisian leadership was soon busy disarming the less prosperous (and hence allegedly more unreliable) elements of its new "National Guard". It appointed the noble patriot Lafayette as its commanding general, to keep any radical tendencies firmly in check. Similar patterns appeared across the country, where many urban militias were even more concerned about the defence of property and order than the one in Paris.

The widespread rural "Great Fear" of late July was an extension of resistance to rumoured aristocratic plots, but that did not stop many at the

Opposite: The storming of the Bastille by the revolutionaries of Paris on the morning of 14 July 1789.

centre reading it as quite possibly such a plot itself: popular mobilisation as "mere anarchy", fomented to destroy revolutionary control of the country. In August, the National Assembly joyfully abandoned privilege and wrote a *Declaration of the Rights of Man*, but it was also careful to insist that feudal and other rights with a cash value would be compensated, and should be paid until they were formally ended. Respect for law and property are woven through the Declaration. It would be several years before the kind of spontaneous abolition that the peasantry had carried out in the spring of 1789 was recognised as a reality.

The tension between knowing that the Revolution depended on popular support and wishing to stabilise the social structure ran through the following years. Radicals remained willing to see crowds as a legitimate expression of the popular will, while conservatives and centrists tried to build a political nation of property owners and taxpayers. Both groups feared an aristocratic backlash, and each came to see the other as a potential treacherous agent of that "counter-revolution". Here lay many of the Revolution's future troubles.

Why did revolutionary politics become a spiral of violence?

The "problem of violence" in the French Revolution is one that has occupied many historians, but they often overlook a key fact: the "counter-revolution" of aristocratic efforts to destroy the revolution was real, permanent, and based on force. There was a steady drumbeat of news about plans for armed insurrection, only some of which was exaggeration and scare-mongering. Aristocratic emigration started in July 1789 with the king's own brother, Artois, and the *émigrés'* attempts to "save" the king from then on always involved planning either a rising of loyal subjects, or a re-invasion of exiles supported by foreign powers. Counter-revolutionaries may not have been the all-pervasive conspiratorial movement patriots feared, but butchery of the revolutionary leadership was always top of their agenda.

At the highest level, it was clear after the summer of 1789 that belief in Louis XVI's good faith was misplaced. While revolutionary politicians persistently shied away from confronting the monarch, his refusal actually to promulgate the Declaration of Rights and subsequent constitutional outlines was only overcome by the massive Parisian "March on Versailles" in October. Partly born out of reports of the royal family encouraging anti-revolutionary behaviour amongst the military garrison at the palace, this show of popular force left left the king and queen believing that they were now prisoners. Many observers shared the view. The royal couple's transportation to Paris, where the National Assembly quickly joined them, was celebrated as a triumph over a perceived counter-revolutionary enemy.

Within the National Assembly, events like this helped to turn a substantial section of the noble and clerical membership – perhaps over a quarter of the whole Assembly – into an intransigent opposition. Back-pedalling on the abolition of privilege, refusing to accept the new constitution, these men resisted every attempt to move a constructive agenda forward. Many formed their own "clubs", echoing the sociability of patriotic groups, and publicised their resistance. Several of them challenged radical leaders to duels, bringing direct violence into the heart of politics.

In the country at large, nobles continued to resist the end of their privileges, bombarding the government and Assembly with protests against popular actions that continued in the spirit of 1789, and beginning legal proceedings against peasant communities as soon as the Assembly confirmed that feudal dues did, indeed, need to be paid. This resistance built up local patterns of hostility and suspicion and contributed to regional waves of riotous violence that destroyed feudal records, forced renunciations of rights, burned manors and stirred passions on both sides.

Louis XVI and Marie Antoinette, of course, were completely unreconciled to the Revolution. Only days after his forced move to Paris, the king wrote to his cousin, the king of Spain, announcing that he was a prisoner, and denouncing any acts that revolutionary authorities promulgated in his name. A year later, a letter to the emigrated baron de Breteuil (that may in fact have been written by the queen) gave Louis's sanction to anything Breteuil could do to bring foreign powers to his aid. By early 1791, the couple were actively plotting an escape from Paris, an armed seizure of power, and a new "constitutional" settlement that turned the clock back to their pre-revolutionary wishes. Their attempt in June to carry this out, the abortive "Flight to Varennes", was a major turning point in public sentiment, even though the leadership of the Assembly pretended the couple had been kidnapped and were returning of their own free will. [12]

Why was the Revolution seen as an attack on religion?

The perception, from late 1789 onwards, that the Revolution was a plot against Catholicism made counter-revolutionary activity particularly intransigent. The Catholic Church lost its corporate privileges, its right to charge fees for services, and its many feudal sources of income in August 1789. By the end of that year it had also seen its property holdings effectively nationalised, as the Assembly created *assignat* bonds backed by these assets to relieve the state's debts.

Some were always prepared to see the upheaval of the Revolution as connected to conspiratorial groupings that were fundamentally anti-religious, even if they had to invent most of the connections between the Enlightenment, Freemasons, Jews and Illuminati that this reasoning relied on. But the National Assembly's attempt to rationalise a Church structure that now had no independent assets, and was thus dependent on state funding, added real fuel to this at first imaginary fire.

From early 1790, attempts to audit and close down "redundant" monasteries and convents (often with only a handful of residents) met with popular resistance, especially in southern cities where tensions with a Protestant minority were rising. Several violent episodes mixed popular resistance with sectarian hostility, and the active engagement of counter-revolutionary leaders. Most notable was the *bagarre de Nîmes* in June 1790, a so-called "brawl" which was actually three days of street fighting that left several hundred dead. This echoed on into the *camp de Jalès* in August, where as many as 20,000 armed Catholic

National Guardsmen gathered a few day's march from Nîmes, with uncertain aims but in clear defence of their religion.

From the summer of 1790 a new Civil Constitution of the Clergy mandated a complete reorganisation of the Church. More than a third of its bishoprics were to be dissolved; new boundaries were to align with the new civil structures of Departments and Communes; many parishes were to be merged, and all their historic identities lost; monasticism was abolished, and with it, inadvertently, all the structures of healthcare and education that it provided; numbers of priests were to be sharply limited.

Despite the authorities' ongoing protestations that they were simply trying to make the Church more efficient, these measures were widely perceived as harmful to the religious basis of society. In both urban and rural areas there was lively resistance. By later in 1790 this had coalesced into periodic insurrections of the peasantry against any efforts to enforce the new order of things. Determined to win out, the Assembly imposed a loyalty oath on all priests in January 1791. Most bishops, and almost half of all priests, refused it. Some communities expelled their priests – either for oath taking or refusal – while others violently resisted revolutionary outsiders' attempts to remove them.

Helpless in the face of such disruption, the

National Assembly had to allow the oath-refusing ("non-juring") clergy to stay on where there were no immediate replacements available, and to permit even those who had stepped down from official posts the use of other premises for dissident services. Particularly in the west and the southeast, whole regions were now dominated by a non-juring clergy, widely supported by the rest of the population. Urban revolutionary authorities often felt themselves to be isolated, and sometimes under siege, from this point on. This would feed into the appalling violence of the Vendée revolt two years later.

The oath of the clergy was no less divisive at the centre. Paris was shaken by several episodes of rioting against the non-juring clergy, who made up about half the priests in the city, and further convulsed by rumours that such men's supporters were part of the counter-revolution. The king's aunts caused huge alarm by leaving the city on what was advertised as a pilgrimage to Rome to consult the pope. The king himself caused outrage by taking communion from a non-juror priest on Palm Sunday, and attempting to leave the city for the palace of Saint-Cloud to avoid being forced to hear a public Easter mass from a "constitutional" priest. A massive crowd blockaded the Tuileries palace, preventing his departure, despite the intervention of Lafayette and the National Guard.

What was the effect of suspicion and inflamed passion on both sides?

Radicals were not passive in the face of the counter-revolutionary threat. At the extreme end, the journalist Jean-Paul Marat built up a loyal Parisian following by constantly reiterating the need for a violent purge of compromised figures throughout the political hierarchy to save the Revolution from catastrophic betrayal. Few others went that far, but none disputed that there was danger on every side, or that the power of the state, including armed force, had to be used to defend the new constitution.

In the complex realities of politics, this could lead to tragedy. In August 1790, three army regiments mutinied at Nancy on the eastern frontier, demanding better treatment from their officers. The National Assembly, terrified of losing control of this region vital to national defence, ordered more than 4,000 troops to march on the city. Confrontation with the mutineers broke down into general fighting with some 500 casualties. The officer who led the suppression was a royalist who later emigrated, and radicals over the next year turned the feared mutineers into popular martyrs.

The following summer, Paris was convulsed by alarm at the king's Flight to Varennes and debate about what to do with him. When the National Assembly voted in mid-July to reinstate him, radicals sought to launch a mass petition for a national referendum on the decision. Tensions were running so high between the gathering crowds and the National Guard militia – each attentive to rumours that the other was riddled with counter-revolutionaries – that minor incidents provoked a wholesale confrontation on 17th July. This "Massacre of the Champ de Mars" left more than a dozen dead, and sent the radical leadership into panicked hiding.

In October 1791, conflict over the future of Avignon in the southeast, a historic enclave of papal territory now annexed to France by the demand of some of its inhabitants, produced gruesome bloodshed. Some 60 pro-papal figures were executed by local radicals in revenge for the lynching of a revolutionary official. Debate in Paris on an amnesty for the killers revealed widespread willingness to sanction the bloodiest of deeds, when framed within a narrative of looming counter-revolutionary disaster.

The argument that the Revolution faced deadly enemies was always complicated, as such examples show, by the difficulty of distinguishing between friend and foe. Real, verifiable counter-revolutionary action brought with it a cloud of suspected misdeeds. Thus the falling value of the *assignats* against gold and silver coinage – a real economic issue by 1791, as more and more were printed – was seen as a plot to destabilise the country, rather than an inevitable consequence of inflation.

Politicians tended to interpret panicked popular responses to such problems as stirred up by their enemies, rather than the result of fears spread through the same narratives of counter-revolutionary threat that they themselves subscribed to. By the time the new Constitution finally came into effect in October 1791, every locality had built up its own repertoire of stories of what local "aristocrats" and "fanatics" had done, and how such figures clearly formed part of a larger structure of evil.

Sentiments like this played a strong role in the decision to take France to war in 1792. The agenda of the newly elected Legislative Assembly became dominated by a group of quasi-republican radicals around Jacques-Pierre Brissot, a successful Parisian journalist and politician. By late 1791, these "Brissotins" had forced the king to veto proposed measures against priests and emigrated aristocrats, and embarked on a campaign to rally the country behind the cleansing of the threat of the emigration by war. Their rhetoric positioned the French as the heralds of a new age for all humanity.

The rhetoric of war, as the French used it at this point and later, combined the notion that all good people would – must – greet them as universal liberators, with the conviction that, to achieve a shining future for humanity, it was worth fighting a war without conventional constraints: a war to end war. When they were not greeted as liberators, and when some of the French themselves rose up in resistance to conscription and political divisions, this optimistic vision proved a licence for terrible things.

How did a revolutionary political culture develop?

The people who made the French Revolution had to define what they were doing almost from

**FALLEN IDOLS NO.2
JACQUES-PIERRE
BRISSOT
(1754-1793)**

An innkeeper's son who became a lawyer, journalist and campaigner in the 1780s, Brissot was ideally placed to rise in revolutionary politics. Surviving various questionable business ventures and brushes with the police, he founded a prominent slavery abolition society, the "Friends of the Blacks", in 1788, and a successful newspaper, the *French Patriot*, soon after the fall of the Bastille.

An ardent Jacobin with elite and international contacts, Brissot was an activist in Parisian municipal politics. He took a sharply radical view of events after the Flight to Varennes, and election to the Legislative

scratch. There had been many proposals for reform before, but until the events of the summer of 1789 all of them were essentially grounded in the idea of a secure royal state leading the way hand-in-hand with a unanimous, enlightened "public opinion". The actual situation in which the Revolution's founding texts emerged – a collapse of government, looming state bankruptcy, a new national political class learning to be politicians as they went along, huge popular mobilisations, and huge elite anxiety about what such mobilisation meant – was unthinkable beforehand, and therefore unimagined.

Very quickly, amongst the members of the National Assembly, and across the country, an

---

Assembly saw him lead a "Brissotin" group set on confrontation with the king. The drive to war, however, saw this group making ever-more grandiose claims about French superiority. In the early summer of 1792 Brissot came close to advocating for the monarchy he had condemned a year before, believing its overthrow would lead to chaotic defeat. In more radical eyes this painted him as a traitor.

There was no way back from this, and in the new National Convention Brissot and the relabelled "Girondins" persistently doubled down on their hatred for Robespierre, Marat and "Montagnard" Jacobins, who reciprocated in full. This rivalry drove accelerating political strife until the Girondins' expulsion from the Convention in June 1793. Held in prison after a short-lived escape attempt, Brissot was executed after a show trial in October. ∎

innovative revolutionary political culture developed. It began with the exchange of information, picking up from the waves of letters to the government which had marked the preparations for the Estates-General. Private correspondence, which had often in the past been shared with friends and family, now became for many Assembly deputies a sort of personal newspaper, intended to be read out to anxious groups of fellow citizens, spreading word of what the writers knew (and feared) of events, and often calling for responses, reciprocal local news, and advice.

With the abandonment of royal censorship, the summer of 1789 also saw an explosion of real printed newspapers, sold on the streets of the capital and by subscription across the country, along with pamphlets by the hundreds and eventually thousands, on every conceivable subject. Bookshops, libraries and subscription reading-rooms further swelled as uncertainty created an insatiable demand for news.

These things had a pre-revolutionary existence, but what were formerly the leisurely pursuits of gentlemen, lawyers and merchants now acquired feverish intensity. The capital's open spaces such as the Place de Grève, Palais-Royal and Tuileries Gardens were occupied by permanent crowds who came to exchange information. In the Palais-Royal such groups - gathering, mingling and debating - echoed pre-revolutionary sociability, but with a harder edge of instability and sedition. Around the National Assembly, when it took up its new quarters near the Tuileries palace, there was a constant interchange between those who packed into the public galleries, craning to hear every word, and those outside, of both sexes and every social class, who could only learn what others passed on.

The rumours of the streets, press and private correspondence interacted with each other, sometimes spreading real news with almost supernatural speed, sometimes doing the same with inflated or absurdly paranoid claims. The existence of this ferment itself was hugely troubling. Fear of the potential harm done by "bad" information led to several calls for institutions to be set up to vet news for veracity and credibility. No such machinery, with its clear echoes of an older vision of enlightened leadership and public unanimity, could actually be created, but the paradoxical desire for it continued to echo through the institutions that the revolutionaries did create.

TEN FACTS ABOUT THE FRENCH REVOLUTION

1.
Louis XVI and Marie-Antoinette were a happily married couple, despite much scurrilous rumour to the contrary. A lot of defamatory printed material about the queen had been literally locked up in the Bastille, and was 'liberated' in 1789 to devastating effect.

2.
The drafter of the American Declaration of Independence, Thomas Jefferson, was US ambassador in Paris until September 1789, and advised his friend Lafayette on political tactics. They had already drafted a French 'bill of rights' months before the Declaration of the Rights of Man was debated.

3.
Representatives of the unprivileged 'Third Estate' were supposed to wear a dowdy black uniform for

the Estates-General. Although some tried to claim it as a badge of commoner honour, most refused, and wore fashionable clothes instead.

4.
On the 'Night of 4 August', 1789, when privileges were renounced, some speakers volunteered to give up their own privileges, but others, more spitefully, proposed the removal of those from rival groups in the elite. Ultimately, all went.

5.
During his attempted escape in 1791, the 'Flight to Varennes', Louis XVI was recognised from his profile on an assignat banknote, and detained in the house of a grocer named Sauce – producing many puns on his eating-habits.

6.
Despite the general misogyny of revolutionary politics, French women made breakthroughs in many areas – more female authors published books in the 1790s than had managed to do so in the previous three decades.

7.
Jean-Paul Marat was famously assassinated in his bath in July 1793 – he bathed to relieve a skin disease he had probably caught while hiding in the

Paris sewers, when enraged local authorities in 1790 were seeking to imprison him for libelling them.

8.
From the spring of 1793 to the end of the Terror, the Revolutionary Tribunal in Paris was feared as the scene of death-dealing show-trials, but for the first 12 months of its existence, it acquitted more people than it condemned.

9.
When the so-called 'Thermidorians' turned against Robespierre, they made him into a scapegoat for the Terror by calling him a counter-revolutionary – even claiming he wanted to marry Louis XVI's daughter and have himself crowned, and planting a fake royal seal in his offices.

10.
Literally hundreds of new newspapers started up in Paris between 1789 and 1791: the availability of machines to print them on suggests that there had been many presses hidden from official censors in the city beforehand.

*A founding document of the Revolution,
1789's* Declaration of the Rights of Man & the Citizen

Why were the French so terrified of political dissent?

From top to bottom, French revolutionary political culture was haunted by the vision of unanimity. From their ideas of what a good king should do, how good government should operate and what "public opinion" was, revolutionaries were committed to the idea that an openly oppositional political process was toxic. Frenchmen looked across the Channel to Westminster and saw the British Parliament riven by partisan feuds, corruption, place-seeking and the manipulation of public office for gain. They denounced "faction" – what we might now call open political organisation – at every opportunity, and built into their new

WOMEN AND THE REVOLUTION

The French Revolution was a great liberatory moment for women. Unfortunately, much of that liberation was buried under a thick blanket of misogyny. Women who stood out as individuals in this period tended to have tragic careers.

Olympe de Gouges, a prolific playwright and advocate of social justice, wrote a *Declaration of the Rights of Woman* (1791), and other works advocating freedom and equality for women. Her closeness to the Girondins, and her public denunciation of the decision to execute the king, led to her arrest and execution after she was condemned for "counter-revolutionary" themes

constitution a rigorous separation between the elected representatives of the Nation and the corrupting possibilities of government office.

The revolutionary process committed itself to dissolving all those areas of Old Regime life that had nurtured division. The separate law codes administered by different regional *parlements* were to be rewritten as one, and the *parlements* themselves and many other overlapping, inconsistent structures swept away. The ancient provinces did not merely lose their divisive privileges, but were actually erased from the map, replaced by Departments of uniform size. The sovereignty of the Nation was declared to be absolute, and any divisions within it were purely functional. By 1791 this took a harder social edge,

---

supposedly found in her unpublished writings. A few days later another prominent woman revolutionary, the Girondin muse Manon Roland – also condemned after a token trial – was taken to the guillotine, where she is said to have declaimed: "O liberty, what crimes are committed in thy name!"

For those who were not Girondin sympathisers, the prospect was little better. Claire Lacombe, an actress, and her friend Pauline Léon, a chocolate-maker, were amongst a small group of male and female ultra-radicals labelled the *enragés*, the "mad ones". They led a group known as the Society of Revolutionary Republican Women, and publicly demanded a more militant role for women in defence of the Republic. After a brief heyday in the summer of 1793, they came to be seen by the Montagnards as a dangerous nuisance, leading to the banning of all female

as workers were banned from organising themselves, and instructed that individual agreement was the only acceptable way of discussing their wages and conditions with employers, now that privileged guilds had also been abolished.

When the revolutionaries conceived the voting processes for the new democratic institutions, the expected unanimity of equal individuals cast a strange shadow. Nobody was permitted to declare themselves a candidate for office: to do so, or to publicly advocate for someone else, was made a crime. Taxpaying electors – a majority of the adult males in the countryside, though a much smaller proportion in towns – gathered for local electoral assemblies that sometimes went on for days, and were called to make a private reflection on the

---

political groups in October. Both Lacombe and Léon disappeared into obscurity after spells of imprisonment in 1794.

But these unhappy stories should not obscure an important point about the Revolution. Women made up half the population, and on every occasion where crowds engaged in collective action they were there alongside men. Right through the rise and fall of the sans-culotte movement in Paris, despite the misogyny of its leadership, women were notable amongst the rank and file – after their last risings in the spring of 1795, in ironic testimony of this, they were banned from gathering in groups of more than five on the streets of Paris.

Women were equally prominent in opposing revolutionary ways. Thousands of them were the faithful followers of the Vendean army, and perished alongside men in its defeat

individuals whose personal qualities best suited them for public office – sometimes in lists of dozens – and name them on their ballots.

What this system created was an arduous process, repeated more than half a dozen times for different layers of government in 1790-91, within which early enthusiasm soon faded to the participation of a small minority. In many places, from villages to quite significant towns, an existing dominant grouping simply took power. In others, local factions which had been bitterly divided before 1789 continued to be so afterwards, sometimes with greater violence. Meanwhile, as new forms of sociability and political engagement grew, the fundamental belief that politics was a field of virtuous unanimity created more and more problems.

– a few actually fought in men's clothing in the front lines. No revolutionary authorities ever seriously considered giving women a vote, but they were a force to be reckoned with throughout.

If we step away from strife, we can also see the female role growing in the 1790s, with women becoming published authors on every conceivable subject, in much higher numbers than previously. By their thousands, women were able to take advantage of new laws on divorce and inheritance, gaining recognition as individuals with civil rights, if not political ones. The backlash came later as social practices turned elite women once more into ornaments of salons, and Napoleon's legal code drove all women back into a condition of legal subordination from which it would take much of the next century to escape. ■

Who were the Jacobins?

In this space, between the fear of government power, the dread of counter-revolution, and the belief in a united nation of equal citizens, the Jacobin movement was born. Initially, late in 1789, it was a gathering of the small minority of National Assembly deputies most committed to resisting royal power and the counter-revolutionary threat. At first their meetings were anxious and defensive, but by the beginning of 1790 they had opened their membership to non-deputies (though keeping a subscription fee that confined access to the prosperous). They agreed an agenda of debating political issues prior to the Assembly, pressing forwards to consolidate the gains of 1789, and corresponding with like-minded provincial groups. In a modern context, this would clearly represent a political caucus, the kernel of an emergent political party. Jacobinism's resistance to that implication was one of its great strengths, but also, eventually, a huge weakness.

The formation of "clubs" (the French borrowed the English word directly) accelerated across France from 1790, as it became clear that the constitution-making process was not going to settle down quickly into any simple new normality. In dozens, and by the year's end hundreds, of localities, men of the property-owning and educated classes came together, often seeing themselves as the natural leaders of the new

Nation being created, to debate the local implications of national developments and, through correspondence and delegations, to bind themselves into that national process.

In most places there was only one club, but in some – such as Bordeaux – there were several, simultaneously acknowledging sectional divisions and claiming patriotic unanimity. In Lyon, France's second city, a network of neighbourhood clubs formed, reaching down to the class of craftsmen in the city's dominant silk trades. In Paris, club formation in the shadow of the original Jacobins was rather more patchy. One major club, the Cordeliers, formed in May 1790, reached out to a lower social class with cheaper subscriptions, and by early 1791 there were perhaps ten or a dozen "popular societies" formed in various neighbourhoods. Both the Jacobins and Cordeliers took their names from the nationalised monastic buildings in which they met, as did several others.

Identifying themselves explicitly as the "Friends of the Constitution", the Jacobins hovered ambiguously between stating that they were merely such friends (with no other agenda), and implying that they were the *only* such friends (and all other groupings were thus counter-revolutionary). The more conservative Assembly deputies and others who formed a "Society of Friends of the Monarchical Constitution" at the end of 1790 strongly resisted the latter claim, with the result that they were immediately branded by radical Parisian newspapers as counter-revolutionaries.

By the end of its first year, the French Revolution had developed a complex and intense political culture, but it was one that shied away from almost all the implications we associate with "politics". The press rang with a massive range of ideological positions, but their arguments were framed in an atmosphere of fear – fear of real or imagined conspiracies and of being denounced for plotting against the Revolution. Organised groups had to deny they were organised, while attacking others for being so. Policy agendas had to be articulated in terms of a very narrow set of assumptions about virtuous

**FALLEN IDOLS NO.3
GEORGES JACQUES
DANTON
(1759-1793)**

Danton was making his way in Paris as a lawyer in 1789, and at first had only a local political role in his neighbourhood district of the Cordeliers. The Cordeliers club that formed there in 1790 became a springboard for radical activism, launching a number of sans-culotte careers. It sent Danton to an administrative role in the Paris municipality from late 1791, to behind-the-scenes engagement in the overthrow of the king the following August, and then, in a meteoric rise, to Minister of Justice immediately afterwards.

Questions over responsibility for the September Massacres began a pattern of mutual hostility between Danton and the Girondins. This continued when Danton resigned his ministry to enter the Convention, where he sat with the Montagnards and

citizenship, while debate – whether in the clubs, the press, or the streets – was characterised by speakers or writers asserting the wickedness of anyone who disagreed with them.

Why was the language of the revolution so extreme?

The revolutionaries were the products of a "culture of calumny", argues the historian Charles Walton. It is an incisive label. For decades before 1789, the effective absence of real public debate, and the conduct of political opposition through

became a leading orator. He spent late 1792 and early 1793 on a mission to the conquered Belgian territories, where rumours of sticky fingers first began to circulate; he returned in time to advocate for the creation of the Revolutionary Tribunal in March 1793, and to sit for four months on the Committee of Public Safety, leaving shortly before Robespierre joined.

After this he had no further administrative roles, though he deployed his oratory on a number of occasions. Unwell for several months, he returned to the Convention at the end of 1793 disillusioned with accelerating purges and de-Christianisation, and began to advocate for moderation, even peace – what Robespierre condemned as "indulgence".

His name became associated with allegations of financial dishonesty and treason and, trapped by an unwillingness to abandon his friends, he seemed weary of life. He rallied briefly to declaim against the worst abuses of evidence and process at his trial in April 1794, but went to the guillotine resigned and cynical. ■

gossip and plotting at Court on the one hand, and illegally-circulated printed matter on the other, had encouraged a language of outrageous insult and defamation. As nobody had to put their name to anything, there was no penalty for lack of restraint, nothing to be gained by not making the most defamatory accusations, and a great deal to be gained, in terms of rapidity of circulation and currency, in making such accusations as vivid as possible.[13]

While contemporaries raged about the power of calumny – a crime, some said, akin to murder, but practised on reputations rather than bodies – they indulged in it without restraint. Some of the bestselling works of the century had retailed sordid fantasies about the Court of Louis XV as fact (though there were plenty of well-attested sordid facts available), and right through the "pre-revolution" rumours about the political ambitions and compromises of senior figures led the gossip in circulation. Historians once thought that Marie Antoinette had been bombarded with defamatory publications before 1789, but it now appears that government officials had been mostly successful in suppressing them (at considerable cost in bribes). After 1789, however, the old material was rediscovered and launched on an avid public.

Claims about royal sexual and other deviances were only a small corner of the general problem of calumny. Members of the National Assembly hurled vile insults at each other, a practice which led to demands for disciplinary laws on the one hand, and duels on the other. The press, on both left and right, spared no effort in inventing new libels. Royalists enjoyed a paper called *Acts of the Apostles*, which used an array of high-cultural, historical and religious references to mock radical patriots relentlessly. Radicals had, amongst others, Marat's *Friend of the People*. Marat specialised in rolling all levels of officialdom into a counter-revolutionary conspiracy, linking it with personal dishonesty and immorality in a fashion that saw him pursued more than once by the Parisian authorities.

Among the calumnies were satirical or demeaning nicknames. Some were simple: counter-revolutionaries in the National Assembly were dismissed as "noirs" (blacks), the nickname deriving both from the colour of clerical dress and from general associations with evil.

Marat called Lafayette "Mottié", a demeaning version of his family name Motier, because "Lafayette" was an aristocratic title, a distinction the Revolution had abolished. The word "Jacobins" itself was at first a scornful reference, being an informal nickname for the order of monks whose building they used. But, as is often the case (with both Whig and Tory in British history, for example), what was meant as an insult soon became a badge of pride.

Throughout the Revolution, indeed, labels were

created which reflected how opponents wanted to see a group rather than what the group actually represented. One exception to this is the Montagnards or "Mountain Men". There may have been some hint of mockery about the first use of this reference to radicals taking the high seats in the Legislative Assembly and Convention, but it was almost at once taken up as an affirmation of their positive values. The writings of Rousseau and others had taught the French to associate mountain regions with sturdy independence and virtuous souls, and these were exactly the qualities Montagnards chose to project.

Most labels, however, including that of the Brissotins (later Girondins), and of the "factions" such as Dantonistes and Hébertistes, were created for the purposes of defining a group against the political mainstream. The practices of nicknaming and calumny met and merged with the compulsion towards unanimity. To belong to a named group, unless it had acquired the special halo of one like the Montagnards, was to be at odds with the patriotic national body to which everyone ought to belong. Hence, by that very act of naming, a group was defamed with a charge it could not answer, except to deny it was a group. It was a trick that continued to be used right through the Revolution.

Opposite: The French singer Chenard in the costume of a sans-culotte at the Festival of Liberation of Savoy, 14th October 1792, by Louis Leopold Boilly.

Who were the "sans-culottes"?

Another partial exception to the rule that labels were demeaning is the "sans-culottes". This term became so useful to revolutionary politicians that its meaning expanded beyond any relation to its initial sense. Michael Sonenscher has traced the origins of the phrase to an arcane jibe about writers who, decades earlier, might have received gifts of cloth to make breeches (*culottes*) from noble patronesses. As it came back into use after 1789, its status as either insult or badge of pride was quite unstable. Literally meaning "without breeches", it could be read scornfully as an attack on poverty. It could refer either to the common people, or to politicians who courted their favour. Between 1792 and 1793, however, it underwent a dramatic transformation, and was taken up as a defiantly *un*-ironic label for the common people (who in fact often did wear breeches, but were increasingly depicted in revolutionary visual culture in a long-trousered version of workers' clothing).[14]

Having become a label for patriotic members of the common people, the term sans-culottes was attached, in particular, to urban political activists, and to a distinctive kind of aggressively vulgar masculinity. This was assisted by the journalist Jacques-René Hébert, whose radical newspaper used a stock stage character, the furnace maker

Père Duchesne, to voice profane commentaries on public events. In a further twist, those who presented themselves as leading sans-culottes were often far from being poor and humble: many activists had been prosperous craftsmen, quite a few were merchants and lawyers, some were even noble in origin.

By the height of the Terror in late 1793 and early 1794, sans-culotte had ballooned into meaning virtually any member of the common people who was sufficiently patriotic not to be suspected of criminal indifference or treachery. It was used routinely in this fashion in political speeches and administrative correspondence. But it was also attacked, notably by Robespierre, as a pantomime mask behind which aristocrats could hide. This was the charge that sent the Hébertistes to the guillotine that spring. What it never consistently meant – though it has often been used since by historians to mean – is any clearly identifiable social class.

The Terror

How many people were actually executed?

Separating myth and reality in the Terror is a complex task. The imagery of the guillotine, of the execution of essentially innocent people, and of bloodthirsty mobs, is so dominant that a real effort is needed to get at the facts. There is plenty of horror in those facts, even if less than is often imagined. We have to grasp both that thousands did die under the guillotine, but also that those thousands were not the tens and hundreds of thousands that later myth suggested. We must also grasp that executions occurred in the wider context of the Terror as a brutal civil war in which hundreds of thousands *did* die.

The Revolutionary Tribunal in Paris was responsible for sending people to the guillotine in the capital. It was the scene of a range of dramatic show trials, all of which were essentially foregone conclusions. By the last months of its operation in the summer of 1794, it was passing hundreds of sentences a week, most of which were for executions.

But it is nonetheless also true that of 680 individuals who went before it in the revolutionary spring month of Prairial, Year II, 164 were acquitted; and of 1,005 in the summer month of Messidor, 208. The court had not begun to hear more than 100 cases a month until the previous autumn, and it was only in the early spring month of Ventôse that condemnations had, for the first time, exceeded acquittals. Back in the summer of 1793, upwards of two-thirds of all cases before the Tribunal had been acquittals. Overall, from its foundation in April 1793 to the fall of Robespierre, the Tribunal pronounced 2,585 death-sentences, 1,306 acquittals, and 130 miscellaneous other sentences, including 36 deportations.[15]

In the latter months of its existence, the Tribunal convicted dozens upon dozens of people on what we can only regard as ludicrously flimsy evidence – vicious anonymous denunciations, reports from agents within the prisons who fabricated plots to save their skins, crude assertions of political malice based on social identities – and it also acquitted dozens upon dozens of others. In the minds of prosecutors, judges and jurors, there were evidently sufficient grounds for deciding guilt and innocence in a fairly systematic fashion. Those grounds emerged from the fraught reality of the war and civil war around them, and from the oppressive reality, as they understood it, of the encircling counter-revolutionary plot.

It was in the context of civil war and counter-revolution that the vast majority of deaths in the Terror occurred. Some 16,500 people were tried and executed across the country as a whole, perhaps as many as 30,000 more were killed without trial as captured rebels when the

Federalist and Vendean Revolts were suppressed. In the course of the revolt in the Vendée, it is estimated that perhaps 200,000 died, including up to 50,000 on the "republican" side, in situations that ranged from open battles and ambushes, to massacres of civilians on both sides, to starvation and epidemic disease.

In grasping this, we again have a delicate balance to strike. Rebels-in-arms were traditionally executed without much ceremony. Louis XIV's troops had done it to Protestant rebels in the 1710s, British troops did it to rebellious Irish in 1798, and those who rose up knew they were entering upon a merciless struggle. Little that the revolutionaries did was outside a long-term pattern of what could happen in such a conflict. Direct casualties of revolutionary violence and civil war may have amounted to 1% of the population. England lost nearly 4% of its population in its 17th-century civil wars, while the parallel, far more ruthless conflict in Ireland may have seen a 40% loss of population: more than 600,000 dead. Napoleon's Grand Army, marching on Moscow in 1812 in pursuit of a mad vision of Continental domination, suffered more casualties than all of France in 1793-94.

What this allows us to say is not that the killings of the Terror were right, or excusable, but that they are not *exceptionally* inexcusable. They occurred in a context of armed conflict, in an era when such conflicts routinely resulted in appalling casualties.

The deaths of the Terror have traditionally been treated differently to those of more "normal" wars, precisely because the sort of social changes the Revolution sought to bring about have traditionally been rejected by those who see international wars, with all their horror, as normal and acceptable.

Can the violence be blamed on the bloodthirsty crowd?

Placing most of the Terror's casualties firmly in the camp of civil war, and thus under conditions of organised military force, is important in correcting another myth: that of the mob as an indiscriminate death-dealing force. Contemporary elite observers and 19th-century critics of revolution drew great comfort from the notion that the experience of 1789 and after proved the danger of allowing common people to interact with politics. George Rudé in the 1950s was one of many Marxist historians who worked to disprove, with detailed evidence, claims about the brutality of "crowds". However, the collapse of Marxism as a global force in the 1980s brought with it a revival of often quite stark claims about evil popular violence, notably in the work of Simon Schama.[16]

Undoubtedly, the explosion of ordinary people into political activity was a stunning shock to the elite of the 18th century. The thought of the "servant classes" rising up and having opinions sent the same sort of tremor through them as present-day science fiction alarms that our cars and domestic appliances might one day develop into a robot rebellion. Yet employers of servants were already deeply distrustful of them long before the Revolution. Much of the fear of crowds in the 1780s and 1790s reflected pre-existing mixtures of disdain and dread.

Attention to the occasional violence of collective activity has obscured how much of it was not directed at doing harm. The recent work of Micah Alpaugh has highlighted that Paris saw literally hundreds of popular gatherings, marches and protests in the years before the Terror, and that most of them had no violent intent or outcome. Some did, of course, and Parisian crowds, like those in many other parts of the country, put to death individuals from high officials to lowly thieves, from the very start of the Revolution.[17]

Although some intellectuals had begun quietly to question the death penalty, and the overt cruelty of judicial torture had been abolished a (very) few years before, French people in 1789 lived in a culture where judicial execution was perfectly legitimate, and such executions were often intended to be both painful and spectacular. The state jealously guarded its monopoly of the justice system that handed down such sentences, but when state power fractured – by definition, what happens in a revolution – crowds, in a limited number of critical situations, seized what they saw as the necessity to determine justice for themselves.

Meanwhile, revolutionary politicians themselves had complex attitudes to popular violence, especially when it threatened their freedom of action (or indeed their lives). In the days after the grim "September Massacres" of 1792 in the Parisian prisons, there was near-consensus that this had been a regrettable necessity. But as tensions between Girondins and Montagnards rose in the following weeks, the Massacres came to be seen by the former as a Montagnard plot to destroy them. In the next months, politicians generally came to see controlling popular initiative as a critical issue: when in March 1793 the Revolutionary Tribunal was created, Danton famously declared: "Let us be terrible, so that the people does not have to be!"[18]

Most of the legislative and administrative apparatus of the Terror was about control, about using the authority of being Representatives of the People to outweigh the actions and wishes of smaller groups of actual people. Regimentation played a much larger role in events in 1793 and 1794 than crowd initiative. Even the sans-culotte movement, examined closely, worked through organised channels and sometimes surprisingly well-off local office-holders. Politicians at local and national levels often used the threat of force from grimly plebeian followers to coerce the wealthy, but kept that threat on a tight rein most of the time.

By the height of the Terror, most ordinary people who were contributing to public life were doing so as either soldiers under military discipline, or workers in the bureaucratised war economy. They were banned from taking action to protest their conditions, under threat of being branded counter-revolutionaries. Many of the guillotine's victims in this later stage were random collections of ordinary people, their dissent converted into treason by denunciation. The extent to which the most apparently radical phases of the Terror were disconnected from popular wishes is shown by the joy with which both Hébert's and Robespierre's executions were greeted by crowds.

What role did Robespierre play?

The death of Robespierre and his close ideological companions is rightly seen as ending "the Terror" – but this is mostly because those who killed him used the opportunity to invent the label, and pin it on him. By turning on Robespierre they tried to stop a tightening spiral of denunciation at the heart of the national political elite. He seemed a perfect scapegoat, carrying their political sins off into the after-life, allowing them (so they hoped) to make a fresh start. Few stones were left unturned in vilifying him, from rewriting the record of his physical appearance into a collection of sub-human tics and grimaces, to proposing in all

Depiction of the storming of the Tuileries Palace on 10 August 1792

seriousness that he planned to marry Louis XVI's daughter and crown himself king.

Robespierre's role as bogeyman, dominant in right-wing accounts, produced the inevitable reaction of casting him as a hero for the left, with many, from the 19th century onwards, seeing him as a stern, righteous and self-sacrificing revolutionary leader. Victor Hugo depicted 1830s' student revolutionaries modelling themselves on him in *Les Misérables*, and real revolutionaries actually did so in 1848.

Arguments about who was the greater republican hero, Robespierre or Danton, ran through early 20th-century French historiography. For the last half century, although analyses have broadened and deepened our understanding, they have not necessarily clarified it. The Scottish writer Thomas Carlyle in the 1830s dubbed Robespierre the "Seagreen Incorruptible"; one recent collection of essays asks whether he has become the "Seagreen Incomprehensible".[19]

Robespierre took on different guises through the Revolution. In its early years, he rose from obscurity by positioning himself – with absolute sincerity, as far as one can tell – as a fearless defender of popular liberty; denouncing counter-revolution on all sides and offering himself up as a martyr in the cause of exposing it. He maintained this pose from outside the Legislative Assembly, resisting the urge to war and earning the enmity of the Girondins. Many scholars see him as exhibiting considerable political skill in the period after the fall of the monarchy, controlling the elections from Paris to the Convention. Yet he fades from sight as the king's trial unfolds and the violent dispute between the Girondins and Montagnard/sans-culotte alliance reaches its height in early 1793. He was also conspicuously passive as the Convention was purged at gunpoint in May.

When Robespierre joined the Committee of Public Safety in July 1793, it was a return to his earlier role as fearless and virtuous speechmaker: in a sense, to lend moral authority to the complex task of managing the civil and external wars. While others, notably in the sans-culotte movement, pressurised the Convention into more radical measures in August and September 1793, Robespierre was most visible in defending the Committee against criticisms of its handling of various crises. Through the late autumn and winter he spoke out against excessive radicalism in the form of "de-Christianisation", and also, ominously, gave attention to unfolding rumours of corruption at the heart of politics. With his own conspicuously modest and virtuous life on display, this was an area he could ferociously condemn.

In early 1794, he made several major speeches setting out a middle way of revolutionary virtue and purity between what he viewed as dangerously compromising calls for peace, and suspiciously inauthentic sans-culotte calls for insurrection. Yet at the same time it was others who took the lead in driving Hébertistes and Dantonistes to the guillotine. It is only really from the spring of 1794 that his ideas began to have a real impact. He was essentially responsible for inventing the "Cult of the Supreme Being" which steered a middle way between Catholicism and de-Christianised atheism and led to a flurry of moves to reform French culture.

It was in the spring, too, that Robespierre took on a proper administrative task for the first time. A "Bureau of General Police" was created to watch over public officials, and he was charged with drawing up lists of patriotic personnel for new roles. His biographer John Hardman paints this period as one of the consolidation of a "Robespierrist" party. This grouping was an increasingly haphazard assemblage of old acquaintances, friends-of-friends, colourless time-servers and groups aligning themselves with Robespierre's notions of persecuted virtue. It was from this atmosphere that the infamous Law of 22 prairial emerged, accelerating the work of the Revolutionary Tribunal, as did the plans to purge the Convention that Robespierre announced on 8 Thermidor, inadvertently paving the way for his own execution.[20]

The biographer Peter McPhee has highlighted the extent to which Robespierre spent at least some of these months prostrated by nervous illness, spending more time, when he was fit, at the Jacobin Club (by now a thoroughly purged echo chamber for his views) than in the more fraught atmosphere of the Convention, or indeed the Committee of Public Safety. His actions on 8 Thermidor clearly show, however, that he thought he was still in a commanding position, even if he was swiftly and almost unanimously proved wrong.[21]

However we judge Robespierre's responsibility for the acceleration of executions in the Terror's final weeks – and he was certainly at the heart of that initiative – we cannot see him as the demonic mastermind behind the whole Terror, still less as the aspirant monarch the Thermidorians denounced him as being. Responsibility for everything that happened in those chaotic, horrific months was spread far more widely.

Why is the pace of events so significant?

Those leading France by 1793 had experienced years of counter-revolutionary threats, alarmism, conspiracy-theorising, real betrayals, and deadly dangers, before arriving at the situation of civil war and external invasion that prompted the Terror. In these chaotic circumstances as they strove to assert control in the name of the "one and indivisible Republic", events spiralled with extraordinary rapidity.

Barely six months passed between the creation of the Revolutionary Tribunal with the support of the Girondins, and its use to send their leaders to the guillotine. Barely six months passed between the sans-culotte movement's success in pushing for a Mass Levy, a Maximum, and other measures of radical mobilisation, and the passage of their most prominent Parisian leaders under the same death-dealing blade. From the summons to national unity represented by the Mass Levy, to the first sweeping purges of office-holders no longer sufficiently "pure", was a period of barely four months. From the apparent triumph of

"Robespierrism" in disposing of "factions" endangering the Republic, to Robespierre's death, was again, a period of barely four months.

Were those responsible for these initiatives simply caught up in events beyond their control? Of course not. Without question they had all accepted that, engaged in a deadly struggle, they had to implement ruthless solutions to survive. Believing they had faced a tentacular and nearly-successful counter-revolution since 1789, they willingly viewed each new setback as a betrayal, and leapt on evidence of corruption at the core of politics as proof that such lack of virtue must be treasonous.

Yet the dizzying speed of political evolution is by no means irrelevant. It distinguishes a man like Robespierre, still passionately advocating against the death-penalty in 1791, and dead three years later, from a man like Stalin, with a long career as a professional revolutionary (and bank robber) behind him by 1917, and decades of ruthless power politics to follow. Russian revolutionaries acted in the context of a well-understood ideological framework, and with a considered willingness to use violence over the long term. French revolutionaries had scarcely a moment to draw breath, and only ever managed the faintest sketches of the future society they hoped for, because throughout the Terror and beyond their focus was on immediate survival. By the summer of 1794, they were sending people to the guillotine for reasons we can see clearly as ridiculous, but they did not have the luxury of time (as we have had) to reflect on why that was.

After The Terror

Did the "real" revolution end in 1794?

It was once quite common to end books on the French Revolution with the fall of Robespierre, or, at most, to give a few pages over to the later 1790s as a sort of lull before Napoleon. For writers on the left, this marked the perception that the end of the Terror was also the end of any effort to make something constructive out of revolutionary circumstances. Having coloured the Revolution as a march of accelerating radicalism towards social equality and a political role for the common people, the abrupt reversal of this apparent trend made the following years uninteresting.

For those on the right, seeing the Revolution as a descent into chaos, the well-deserved death of Robespierre, followed by the slackening of the guillotine's operation and the stifling of any prospect of structural change, was also the end of the story – one towards which, for example, Simon Schama's *Citizens* gallops ever-faster, before stopping almost literally dead.

If we imagine that the "real" French Revolution was embodied in Robespierre and his close associates – which he certainly did, proposing in his last moments of freedom to call the armies to his aid "in the name of the French people" – then stopping at Thermidor makes sense. Rather obviously, however, most of those still alive by the fateful day had a different view. For them what was ending was a stifling cloud of uncertainty, a vortex of confusion in which words (such as sans-culottes) had become disconnected from reality. Thermidor was the end of a period in which the revolutionary political elite had become terrified of itself. With the major zones of civil war essentially (and brutally) pacified by the end of the previous winter, most recent casualties of the Terror had been either the direct result of that elite turning on itself, or tragic collateral damage from wildly spiralling plot accusations.

For most of those who went on the record in the weeks after Thermidor, there was a genuine drive to retrieve the promise of the Revolution and Republic, and a belief, however hedged about by improbable tales, that Robespierre had been leading them to destruction. Now, with the military situation decisively turned in their favour they thought they could draw breath, and remember their underlying purpose. What they came to discover was that such a purpose continued to require drastic action.

There were fine speeches on 9 Thermidor and after, but 10 Thermidor saw the largest batch of victims sent to the guillotine on any one day – "Robespierrists" all. A whole series of measures broke the stranglehold of a small group of representatives on government, creating rotating committee memberships, ensuring a wider base of groups to oversee the government and sweeping away the draconian Law of 22 Prairial. Despite some fine speeches, however, the Convention remained notably confused over how else to act. Five days after executing Robespierre, it banned all nobles and priests from public office; then rescinded the ban the next day. By the end of that week, suspects were being released en masse from prison, sometimes regardless of why they had been sent there.

Mere confusion soon took a darker turn. Before the end of the summer, speeches in the Convention had turned to attacking the more radical survivors of the old Committee of Public Safety, while as the revolutionary "Year II" approached its close at the autumnal equinox, the Jacobin Club expelled leading figures who had taken such an anti-radical turn, and began to campaign for the renewed hardening of all the "terrorist" measures relaxed the month before. Political and social divides which had been suppressed by the "rule" of Robespierre flared into life across the nation.

Why was there a revival of ideological conflict after Thermidor?

Ironically, a social reaction against lower-class influence in politics was probably clearer in these months than any specific political or ideological movement. On the streets of Paris, well-dressed gangs of the "Gilded Youth" attacked Jacobins sporadically, but harassed those of humble origins systematically. By the end of 1794 popular militants were being purged from local authorities, while on 24th December – as a cruelly harsh winter was already biting – the Maximum was abolished, along with all efforts to control supplies beyond a meagre official bread-ration.

Thus, as the Republic continued to enjoy military success, many of its people experienced famine. Amidst the chaos, there can be no definitive accounting, but certainly thousands, perhaps tens of thousands, starved to death. Millions clung on, suffering, while at the pinnacle of politics the "good life" was returning for the elite. Twice the following spring, in the revolutionary months of Germinal and Prairial, Parisian crowds rose up in protest, but were faced down with superior force. All they produced was an enhanced rhetoric of the dangers from popular "terrorists", further repression, and the arrest of new groups of surviving Montagnards.

This atmosphere emboldened those, especially in the southeast, who were unrepentant royalists, and a surge of violent revenge, later labelled a "White Terror", ran through cities from Lyon to Marseille. Massacres of hundreds of Jacobin activists, often within the prisons where they were already confined, ensured that politics in this region continued to be anchored in vendetta for the rest of the decade. Whatever ended at Thermidor, it was certainly not the capacity of revolutionary politics to generate violent conflict.

Meanwhile, in June 1795, Louis XVI's young son, "Louis XVII" to his supporters, wasted away in a Paris prison. From exile in Verona, the new Louis XVIII (brother and uncle of his predecessors) declared that he still planned to return, still intended to restore the pre-1789 social order, and definitely still intended to execute all those who had voted for his brother's death. Despite the Thermidorians' visible turn to the anti-radical right, it was also clear that there could be no easy compromise with those who opposed the Revolution itself.

With royalism a real and enduring threat, the Convention drafted a new republican constitution that offered the checks and balances of an ideal liberal structure, though one which would be manned, mostly, by themselves. A "Law of Two-Thirds" passed at the end of August reserved that proportion of seats in the new assemblies for outgoing Convention members, securing them from the threat of an immediate takeover by their enemies. The fact that it seemed to scorn the very democratic principles it claimed to safeguard was less important to the Thermidorians than the risk of allowing free elections.

A week before the planned ballot for the one-third of seats available in early October, royalists at the heart of Paris staged a demonstration that threatened to turn into a violent insurrection. They were suppressed by loyal troops led by a certain young General Bonaparte. With the Jacobin Club closed down by the Gilded Youth almost a year before, and more recent measures shutting down the popular societies and sectional assemblies that had housed the sans-culottes, the new "Directorial" regime entered into power based on the suppression of enemies to both right and left. The structural balancing act of the new constitution rested on a far more dangerous political balancing act: one that rapidly proved impossible to sustain without further violence.

What did the Directory actually achieve?

The Directory was led by men who were, above all, political survivors. Alongside several solidly centrist time-servers, the first five-man "Executive Directory" included Lazare Carnot, the most hard-nosed and practical member of the Terror's Committee of Public Safety. Also on it, and the only man to remain in post for the full duration of this regime, was Paul Barras. A former nobleman and military officer, he had, as a member of the Convention, ruthlessly repressed Federalist resistance in the southeast during the Terror, then taken a leading role in overthrowing Robespierre. He had been equally energetic in directing General Bonaparte against the royalists of Paris. His vision, like that of those around him, was of a republican state that could consolidate the individual freedom won in 1789, seeing off the threat of a royal restoration by resisting a slide into anarchy.

The positive side of this vision was a re-animation of France as a nation of culture, industry, and scientific excellence: a great nation, or indeed "the Great Nation", to use a label applied often in the later 1790s. The disruption of the previous five years had swept away all the structures of "aristocratic" support for higher learning and culture built up under the monarchy. The Directory embraced the new Institute of Sciences and Arts created in August 1795, bringing together older Academies of the fine arts and literature along with one of science, and a new creation, the Academy of Moral and Political Sciences. This last was to unite philosophy, history, and all that would later become "social science". Its clear mission was to place the expertise of an elite at the heart of a science of government, and thus to consolidate the long-term future of the Republic. Hundreds of scholars would be given access to funds and facilities to carry on its work.

This apparently virtuous goal was, however, firmly linked to the social evolution of the Directory, and the circles that surrounded it in Paris. Robespierrist virtue was thoroughly out of fashion. The social environment of politics rapidly resumed the appearance of an aristocracy, with splendid costumes, ornate balls and the conduct of business at private parties and salons. An atmosphere of both sexual frivolity and material corruption prevailed. Barras, for example, was one of several very public lovers of Joséphine de Beauharnais, whose aristocratic husband had been executed in the Terror. After him, she attracted the passion of General Bonaparte, whom she married in 1796. There is nothing wrong with a little sexual liberation, but in this context it was associated with a determined and visible pursuit of pleasure funded by the state, and a brutal indifference to the suffering so many experienced in the winter of 1794/5.

After the Terror, and the Germinal/Prairial risings, the Directorial elite became firmly committed to the notion that the popular classes were simply unworthy of political consideration. Their new academic institutions produced intellectual rationales for this, imagining the processes of political education that might raise up at least some of the ignorant mass – one day, but definitely not now. The structures of knowledge and the institutions of education were effectively defined as fortifications around the rule of groups which had risen, by fair means and foul, through both the Old Regime and Revolution. A vision of intellectual progress was, in practice, the effort to freeze in place an arbitrary set of distinctions between the haves and the have-nots.

How did the Directory endure for four years?

The intellectual sphere was not the only place where the Directory sought to freeze society. In 1796 they tried to deal with the continued disastrous inflation of the assignat currency by replacing it with another form of paper money, the value of which collapsed almost instantly. France was pushed back towards reliance on metallic currency effectively by default, only saved from total disaster by a flow of loot from its armies' continued advances. In the same year there were new laws against advocating left-wing or right-wing views on property or politics, new clampdowns on the press, and widespread arrests of radical and royalist conspirators.

The "republican centre" the regime was upholding seemed an increasingly fragile and artificial construction. This was decisively demonstrated in the spring of 1797 during the first of the annual elections intended to underpin the new system. Of more than 200 former Convention members who stood for re-election, barely a dozen were chosen. The new legislature was sharply to the right of the Directory. When it threatened its power, a three-man majority of Directors, led by Barras, organised a coup in early September 1797 with army support, unseating the two other Directors (including Carnot, who had turned sharply rightwards), and more than 170 elected deputies. Policy swung to the left, or more accurately against the right, with new measures against priests and nobles, and further general censorship.

With these actions giving encouragement to more radical forces, the Directory realised it was still threatened from that direction as well. So the following year's elections were rigged in advance, with the authorities actively encouraging splits in local electoral assemblies, and nomination of acceptable candidates by more reliable splinter groups. This allowed them to annul many elections of dangerously left-wing candidates, appointing safer men in their place. By the middle of 1798, therefore, any pretence that genuine movements of opinion amongst the electorate were allowed to affect the holders of power at the centre had been abandoned.

To paint the Directory simply as cynical

manipulators, however, is not entirely fair. Many of the local areas whose elections they disrupted were themselves the prey of factional fighting, where the lines between legality, illegality, and simple brute force had been blurred by years of disruption. The work of Howard Brown has shown the extent to which willingness to submit peacefully to external authority – to pay taxes, to accept court judgments, to surrender criminals for trial – had been shattered. Vengeance and vendetta, often deeply personal and communal, even if cloaked in ideological language, was dangerously close to being the norm by the later 1790s. It is ironic, but nonetheless true, that France's best hope of restored social peace probably did lie in the lash of authoritarian government.[22]

Where did Bonaparte emerge from, and how did he rise so fast?

It is easy, almost too easy, to see the Directory as on course for a military dictatorship from its outset. While the Terror had shredded the already fragile social fabric, it had also created the most effective army of the age, which had already gone on the offensive before Robespierre's fall. Throughout the internal turmoil of the following years, France's grip spread across continental Europe. In 1795, Prussia withdrew from the war in the face of

French aggression, agreeing to "neutralise" all of northern Germany. Spain was forced into a peace treaty, and soon bullied into an alliance. The Netherlands were simply overrun and turned into a satellite "sister republic", alongside the Belgian and Rhineland territories that had been annexed to France itself.

In 1796, as civil authorities wrestled with conspirators, the army's attention was turned on Italy, and the war there with Austria. General Bonaparte's political and social connections to Barras had won him the chance of command, and he used it with devastating flair. The border state of Piedmont was driven into surrender within a few weeks of the start of spring campaigning, as were other duchies further south, and by summer the Papal States and Kingdom of Naples likewise signed armistices. Austrian forces held out longer in the fortress-cities of Lombardy, but further relentless campaigning through the winter drove their rulers to the negotiating table from April 1797. In October this produced a formal peace treaty at Campo Formio, acknowledging France's extensive conquests, and its effective dominance of western Europe.

The stunning effectiveness of French military force had significant political consequences. At a basic level, it secured the survival of the regime not just by defeating threatening enemies, but by taking over rich territories which were unscrupulously looted to fund further military action and to underpin the Republic itself. It also tied the leaders of the Republic to the leadership of the army – still widely used to secure internal order. As in the Old Regime, politicians and generals became interwoven in the new social elite. Political and military ambitions interlocked, creating a context in which General Bonaparte flourished.

The character of Napoleon Bonaparte has such an overwhelming presence in history that the context of his rise can be obscured. He was, of course, a staggeringly successful general, but only the Revolution could have given him the opportunity to demonstrate his skill. Without its disruption, and accompanying quest for successful leaders, he would probably have remained a noble-born but impoverished junior officer far into middle age. As it was, he was only 27 when he began to pacify Italy. He blended restless energy with an ambition driven by typical classical examples from his schooling – Alexander, Caesar – and an equally typical romantic sensibility about destiny and greatness. What others expressed in bad poetry – and Napoleon wrote some of that as well – he was able to turn into political drama.

It was still down to the wider culture of the Directorial Republic to shape Bonaparte's potential. The armies he led through Italy were men recruited during the Terror, and not reinforced since. Only in 1798 did politicians decree the creation of a systematic form of annual conscription, the Jourdan Law, that laid the groundwork for continued strength. This was alongside new measures designed to create a more effective system of taxation and crack down on endemic internal unrest. The authoritarian atmosphere that would mark Napoleonic rule was already well-established before he took power, and by many of the same men who would carry it forward.

The dramatic expedition to Egypt, launched in the spring of 1798, showed this blend of the personal and the structural. Although Bonaparte was a strong advocate, it was also part of a wider plan of the Directorial leadership. Conquering Egypt was a way to destabilise British imperial power impossible in other regions because of the Royal Navy's dominance of the oceans. Accessible now because Britain had withdrawn its Mediterranean fleet in the face of a Franco-Spanish alliance, it suited both the dynamics of the current war, where Britain remained an impervious adversary, and the longer-term plans for global contest. The "Great Nation" rhetoric in increasing use reflected a shift from ideological to imperial concerns. This was further marked (with Bonaparte's enthusiastic agreement) by the despatch to Egypt of an extensive band of scholars, whose researches into ancient Egyptian civilization were intended to establish French intellectuals on the same dominant level as the British scholars then in India.

Napoleon Bonaparte in his official costume as First Consul, after the Brumaire coup of November 1799

Although Bonaparte again showed himself as a vigorous general and canny political player in first conquering and then beginning to administer Egypt, he was still constrained by circumstances. The Royal Navy returned to the Mediterranean to hunt him, destroying his supporting fleet in August 1798 and helping to block his intended advance through the Holy Land in the spring of 1799. Meanwhile, the threat of French Mediterranean dominance brought both Turkey and Naples into the war, followed in the spring of 1799 with renewed hostilities against Tuscany and Austria, who now formed a coalition with Britain and Russia.

By late 1799, France faced drastic dangers. Renewed efforts at conscription and taxation had provoked popular uprisings in, among other places, the new Belgian lands; almost all the extensive conquests and new "sister republics" set up in Italy had been lost to a combination of similar uprisings and Austro-Russian advances. The British joined the attack, landing troops jointly with Russia in the Netherlands and seizing the Dutch fleet at anchor. Bonaparte's personal, and highly questionable, decision to abandon his army in Egypt in late summer, arriving in France in mid-October, showed that he intended to be on the scene for some kind of showdown in the looming crisis.

The political year in France had opened in the spring with more manipulated elections. By June the Directory and legislature were at loggerheads, and two further Directors were purged from office, triggering further purges throughout the administration. A short-lived "neo-Jacobin" movement sprang up in Paris, but by the end of the summer it had been forcibly closed down, as authoritarian centrists drove through yet more measures against both left and right. By the time Bonaparte arrived, the wider military situation had been stabilised by the victories of other generals, but a leading group at the centre of politics had decided enough was enough. Led by the same Sieyès who had asked *What is the Third Estate?* in 1789, the plotters cast about for a figurehead, and found Bonaparte after at least one other general had turned them down.

The new "Consulate" that was established after the *coup d'état* of 18 Brumaire (9th November 1799) would not take long to turn into the personal rule of First Consul Bonaparte, and he would resolutely claim both to embody and close down the Revolution in his own person. But if he had been captured by the Royal Navy as he tried to reach France, the Directory would probably still have been ended by a coup, and an overtly authoritarian elite, largely composed of men who had been in power for years, would still have taken charge.

Isser Woloch has studied in detail the men who made Napoleonic France tick, and found that they covered a remarkably broad political spectrum, but buried their differences in pursuit of personal power, material comfort (great wealth in some cases), and a probably genuine belief that only authoritarian structures could suppress the incessant conflicts unleashed by a decade of Revolution. The man who became the Emperor Napoleon in 1804 was an extraordinary individual, but he did not work alone. [23]

Conclusion

The second decade of the 21st century has already seen a manifesto "in defence of the Terror", and a lengthy narrative account of the French Revolution marketed by the radical publishers Verso as a "people's history", as well as a lively dispute in France about the way the politics of the Revolution are depicted in a video game. [24] Historians have even found themselves arguing about Robespierre's face, and whether a new reconstruction was true-to-life, or a defamatory distortion.[25] There is no sign of agreement about what it all meant.

Wider scholarship on the Revolution is increasingly moving beyond the narrative of events in France. Although they took place thousands of miles away, the conflicts and upheavals in the Caribbean during the 1790s – culminating in a massive slave uprising on Saint-Domingue – cast a baleful shadow over the Revolution. France's

Caribbean colonies were home to well over half a million slaves, a standing affront to the notions of "rights" carried into law in 1789. It was not until long after slaves had effectively won their own freedom that French revolutionaries finally agreed to abolish slavery in February 1794. When, three years earlier, they had been finalising the revolutionary constitution of 1791, they had carefully spelt out that the regime they were creating did not affect the colonies – for that would threaten the very dynamo of French international trade. For the vast majority of revolutionaries, the commitment to "rights" did not extend to ending the system of oppression on which France's global economic position depended.[26]

Recognising this is one step towards understanding the Revolution as part of a global, and unashamedly imperial, European world-view, with repercussions that do not fit easily with a simple message of revolutionary liberation. In the east, for example, French liberatory rhetoric led to hundreds of former Ottoman subjects in Egypt – Muslim, Christian, Egyptian and Syrian – sailing to France with the withdrawing French forces in 1801, believing that they could rely on French goodwill to help them make the case for an Egyptian Republic amongst the diplomats of Europe. Instead, the Napoleonic empire treated them as inconvenient refugees.[27]

Moreover, although in practice Napoleonic

imperialism was confined to the European continent (after a brutal and disastrous attempt to re-enslave the rebels of Saint-Domingue) the regime of the 1800s pondered all kinds of schemes for colonial conquest or re-conquest, including a potential return to Egypt, seizure of the "barbary coast" capitals of Algiers and Tunis, expansion of holdings in West Africa and even the take-over of Madagascar.[28]

If the Revolution was not a decisive break in French imperial ambitions, what, more narrowly, did it mean for the lives of those in France? The British historian Richard Cobb produced a body of work in the 1960s and 1970s that demonstrated with striking examples how little it meant for many, trapped by poverty and shockingly brutal everyday social relations.[29] But the "Cobbist" view needs to be put in perspective.

Statistics may seem as dry as dust beside his colourful tales from the police archives, but the story they tell is more hopeful. The majority of the French population – the peasantry – had laboured under huge burdens in the Old Regime, and thanks to a complex combination of revolutionary ideals and their own rebellious will, were freed from many of them during the 1790s. This changed their lives, and the lives of their children. Fewer than half of French children survived to the age of 15 in the decades before 1789; in the subsequent decades this percentage rose sharply to almost two-thirds.

Within a generation, life expectancy at birth was almost a third higher than it had been before. Revolutionary liberation allowed the peasantry, quite simply, to feed their children better, and keep more of them alive.[30]

This material gain has to be put alongside what the peasantry were made to endure by the Revolution. Viewed with suspicion by successive essentially middle-class and urban regimes, the peasantry were burdened with new taxes and stigmatised for being priest-ridden and less than eager to hand over their crops to hungry towns. Those in the west experienced the loss of extensive economic privileges early in the Revolution, with legislation allowing landlords to add the cost of abolished tithes and feudal dues to their rents. Aggressive urban authorities used armed patrols to enforce their will against priests and communities, and then returned in 1793 demanding conscripts. In this context, the revolt of the Vendée can be seen as something very much more than "counter-revolution". It was an act of popular resistance based on legitimate grievances to which "radical" revolutionaries (still celebrated by radicals today) were fatally blinded by their own narrowness of vision.[31]

Yet we should also remember areas in which the revolutionaries showed striking breadth of vision. They embarked in 1789 on the rewriting of France's entire code of laws, both civil and criminal, and brought to these some of the finest sentiments of

Enlightenment humanitarianism. If they did not go so far as to abolish the death penalty, they debated it seriously, and did away at a stroke with all the humiliating and agonising rituals and punishments that had accompanied it. Lesser punishments were placed on a humane and reforming scale, after trials which introduced juries and representation for the accused. The Terror and later authoritarianism distorted much of this temporarily, but the outlines of what became the enduring "Napoleonic Code" of laws were set down in the early 1790s.

In some respects, the Revolution marked a high point of freedom and justice which was not regained until over a century later. Suzanne Desan has charted in detail how the complex web of family law was untangled in the 1790s. For a brief decade – until Napoleon took a more patriarchal view again – marriage became a voluntary union, its end through divorce recognised as a moral solution to human misery. A wave of unhappy couples used the new law as soon as it came into effect in 1792. Other aspects of reform were more problematic: because the state proclaimed its duty to support illegitimate children, women were barred from suing purported fathers, leaving them no recourse when the state actually proved less generous than its pronouncements. Inheritance was rationalised, and all legitimate children were given rights to parental property – a blow against the "tyranny" of unjust parents, but also something that would result in the excessive sub-division of agricultural holdings over the coming century.[32]

Family law was not the only area in which the Revolution's pronouncements outstripped its ability to deliver. The Montagnard Republic of 1793/94 committed itself to reforming education, but lacked the resources to do so: it would be the 1830s before widespread state primary schooling was introduced – and then only for boys. For the poor, the revolutionary years were a disaster, with only the patchy provision of private charity replacing Church institutions that had been systematically broken down. The practical failure of these years to do anything constructive for the weakest in society is an important corrective to the idea that the radical Republic bequeathed a noble heritage of justice and human rights.[33]

In the end, though, we must return to those human rights, because without the French Revolution there is a real chance that we would never have had the opportunity to cherish them. The French in 1789 brought to political life an ideal of freedom and equality that had never before been expressed so directly, systematically, and universally. Their own ability to live up to it was partial and sometimes deeply compromised by self-interest – whether over massive stumbling blocks like slavery and women's political exclusion, or over the humbler issues of how to vote and on what basis. Their attempt to defend their ideals led them down the road to the Terror, and to the creation of both real horror, and a myth of horror, that made promoting equality almost impossible for decades.

But the flame lit in 1789 burned on, setting alight the souls of radicals, liberals, socialists and revolutionaries all through the 19th century and into the 20th. It offered a humane alternative to other structures and tendencies – militant nationalism, imperialism, the rise of industrial cities and regimented mass-movements, and the lure of "scientific racism" and eugenics. And in a moment of appalling darkness, with Auschwitz on one hand and Hiroshima on the other, it cast its glow across a devastated world, expressing the hope of rebuilding, and giving us the Universal Declaration of Human Rights. Many of its idealistic claims are far from being put into practice, even now. But it is a light that shines not just on who we are, but on who we can be. When we act on the belief that we are all free and equal, then the best of the French Revolution lives on.

ENDNOTES

1. In the new French Republican Calendar, designed to remove all religious and royalist influence from the date system, the twelve months were named according to the natural conditions they corresponded to, e.g. Brumaire (mist), Floréal (blossom) and Thermidor (heat). 27th July 1794 was known as 9 Thermidor, and the term Thermidor came to signify a retreat from radicalism because of its association with the overthrow of Robespierre.
2. François Furet, *Interpreting the French Revolution* (Cambridge, 1981); Keith M. Baker, *Inventing the French Revolution* (Cambridge, 1990), citation p. 305; Simon Schama, *Citizens; a chronicle of the French Revolution* (New York, 1989).
3. Colin Lucas, 'Nobles, Bourgeois, and the Origins of the French Revolution', orig. pub. 1973, reprinted in Gary Kates, ed., *The French Revolution: Recent Debates and New Controversies* (London, 1998), pp. 44-67; citation p. 48. For 'Anglo-Saxon revisionism' in general, see William Doyle, *Origins of the French Revolution* (Oxford, several editions).
4. Colin Jones, 'Bourgeois Revolution Revivified; 1789 and social change', in Kates, ed., *Recent Debates*, pp. 157-91. Lauren Clay, 'The Bourgeoisie, Capitalism and the Origins of the French Revolution', in David Andress, ed., *The Oxford Handbook of the French Revolution* (Oxford, 2015), pp. 21-39.
5. Timothy Tackett, *Becoming a Revolutionary; The Deputies of the French National Assembly and the Emergence of a Revolutionary Culture* (1789–1790) (Princeton, 1996).
6. John Hardman, *Overture to Revolution; The 1787 Assembly of Notables and the Crisis of France's Old Regime* (Oxford, 2010); Vivian R. Gruder, *The Notables and the Nation; The Political Schooling of the French, 1787–1788* (Cambridge, MA., 2008).
7. Antoine Lilti, 'The Kingdom of Politesse: Salons and the Republic of Letters in Eighteenth-Century Paris', *Republics of Letters*, vol. 1, issue 1.

8. Robert Darnton, *The Forbidden Bestsellers of Pre-revolutionary France* (New York, 1995); Simon Burrows, *Blackmail, Scandal, and Revolution; London's French libellistes, 1758–1792* (Manchester, 2006); Louise Seaward, 'Censorship through Cooperation: The Société typographique de Neuchâtel (STN) and the French Government, 1769-89', *French History*, vol. 28 (1), 2014, pp. 23-42.
9. P.M. Jones, *Reform and Revolution in France; the politics of transition, 1734-1791* (Cambridge, 1995).
10. Alexis de Tocqueville, *The Ancien Régime* (everyman edition, London, 1988), p. 114.
11. Cited in David Andress, *1789; the threshold of the modern world* (London, 2008), pp. 210-11.
12. On the authorship of the letter, see Munro Price, *The Road from Versailles; Louis XVI, Marie Antoinette, and the fall of the French monarchy* (New York, 2002), appendix, pp. 369-72.
13. Charles Walton, *Policing Public Opinion in the French Revolution; The Culture of Calumny and the Problem of Free Speech* (Oxford, 2009).
14. Michael Sonenscher, *Sans-culottes; An Eighteenth-Century Emblem in the French Revolution* (Princeton, 2008).
15. Gérard Walter, ed., *Actes du Tribunal révolutionnaire* (Paris, 1968), pp. 29-33.
16. George Rudé, *The Crowd in the French Revolution* (Oxford, 1959).
17. Micah Alpaugh, *Non-Violence and the French Revolution; Political Demonstrations in Paris, 1787–1795* (Cambridge, 2014).
18. Emphasised in Sophie Wahnich, *In Defence of the Terror: Liberty or Death in the French Revolution* (London, 2012).
19. Colin Haydon and William Doyle, ed., *Robespierre* (Cambridge, 1999), p. 3.
20. John Hardman, *Robespierre*, (London, 1999).
21. Peter McPhee, *Robespierre; a revolutionary life* (New Haven, 2012).
22. Howard Brown, *Ending the French Revolution: Violence, Justice, and Repression from the Terror to Napoleon*

(Charlottesville, 2006); see also D.M.G. Sutherland, *Murder in Aubagne; lynching, law and justice during the French Revolution* (Cambridge, 2009).
23. Isser Woloch, *Napoleon and His Collaborators; the making of a dictatorship* (New York, 2001).
24. Sophie Wahnich, *In Defence of the Terror: Liberty or Death in the French Revolution* (London: Verso, 2012); Eric Hazan, *A People's History of the French Revolution* (London, 2014).
25. Discussed by Robespierre biographer Peter McPhee here: < http://www.thelancet.com/journals/lancet/article/PIIS0140-6736(14)60564-X/fulltext>.
26. Jeremy D. Popkin, *A Concise History of the Haitian Revolution*, Malden: Blackwell, 2012; Manuel Covo, 'Race, Slavery, and Colonies in the French Revolution', in Andress, ed., *Oxford Handbook*, pp. 290-307.
27. Ian Coller, 'Egypt in the French Revolution', in Suzanne Desan, Lynn Hunt & William Max Nelson, ed., *The French Revolution in Global Perspective*, Ithaca, NY: Cornell UP, 2013, pp. 115-31, esp. pp. 129-31.
28. Yves Benot, *La démence coloniale sous Napoléon*, Paris: La Découverte, 1992.
29. Richard C. Cobb, *Reactions to the French Revolution* (Oxford, 1972), amongst many works.
30. Paul G. Spagnoli, 'The Unique Decline of Mortality in Revolutionary France', *Journal of Family History*, 22, 1997, pp. 425-61.
31. D.M.G. Sutherland, *The French Revolution and Empire; the quest for a civic order*, Oxford, 2003, addresses this perspective, emergent from his own and others' earlier work, pp. 155-61.
32. Suzanne Desan, *The Family on Trial in Revolutionary France* (Berkeley, 2004).
33. Alan Forrest, *The French Revolution and the Poor* (Oxford, 1981).

GLOSSARY

American War of Independence – between 1775 and 1783, rebels in 13 North American colonies waged a successful war against Britain, seceding from its empire and forming an independent government. France allied with the new nation in this struggle.

Assignats – Originally interest-bearing bonds paid to the state's creditors, and secured on the value of confiscated Church lands, by 1791 they were being used as a paper currency, and suffering inflation that would run out of control after 1794.

Brissotins – named after their most prominent spokesman, Jacques-Pierre Brissot, a loosely affiliated republican group, also known later as Girondins, as some of them originated from the département of the Gironde. They reached the height of their popularity with their support for "revolutionary war" in the spring of 1792, but their influence declined and many were executed as more radical groups came to direct the Revolution's course.

Committee of Public Safety – established in 1793 to provide for the defence of the nation against its enemies, and to oversee the other organs of government. Elected by and from the National Convention from amongst its own membership, it had effectively dictatorial powers during the Terror.

Enlightenment – a European intellectual movement of the 18th century, central to which was the celebration of reason. The objectives of rational humanity were thought to be knowledge, freedom and happiness.

Estates General – the time-honoured representative assembly of the three "estates" or orders of the realm: the clergy (the First Estate), nobility (the Second Estate), and the Third Estate, whose deputies represented the majority of the population. Dormant under the absolute monarchy, it had not met since 1614.

Freemasonry – a secret brotherhood that supposedly evolved from the guilds of stonemasons in the Middle Ages, and was a popular form of sociability amongst French nobles and wealthy elites in the 18th century.

General Maximum – a law, passed in September 1793, which set ceilings on the price of staple goods and laid regulations for how these were to be policed.

Jacobins – (or the Jacobin Club) the most famous revolutionary group, dominated first by the more moderate Girondins and then by the Montagnards. Their time in government from 1793-4 was characterised by very high levels of political violence. With the fall of Robespierre, the club was closed down.

Law of 22 prairial – also known as "the law of the Great Terror" this was passed by the National Assembly on 10 June 1794 to streamline justice, denying the accused any effective right to a defence and eliminating all sentences other than acquittal or death.

Mass Levy – a decree passed in August 1793, requiring all unmarried men between 18 and 25 years to present themselves for military service. This unique concept of a mass citizen army transformed the nature of warfare and other groups to take part in production for a war-economy.

Montagnards – members of La Montagne, the collection of the radical Jacobin deputies who sat on the higher benches in the National Assembly. They opposed the more moderate Girondists and effectively controlled the government in 1793-4, until Thermidor, when many of them were purged.

National Convention – consisting of nearly 750 deputies, it was elected to provide a new constitution after the overthrow of the monarch. It governed France from 1792 to 1795, when it approved the constitution for the new regime that replaced it, the Directory.

Sans-culottes – a term for radical activists that developed in 1791-92, and by the time of the Terror was often used to label the whole body of patriotic common people (see p.83 for further details).

Seven Years' War – lasting from 1756 to 1763, this was the last major conflict before the revolutionary wars to involve all the great European powers. Under the concluding Treaty of Paris, France renounced to Britain huge swathes of territory in North America and India.

Thermidor – also called the Thermidorian Reaction, this was a revolt on 9 Thermidor, Year II (27th July 1794) in the National Assembly. It was primarily a reassertion of the rights of the National Convention against the Committee of Public Safety and resulted in the fall of Robespierre and the collapse of the Terror.

FURTHER READING

General textbooks:
William Doyle, *The Oxford History of the French Revolution* second edition (Oxford, 2002) is a very readable general political narrative of events. It can be complemented with his *The French Revolution; a very short introduction* (Oxford, 2001) as a brief overview. Two solid and relatively brief contributions are Peter McPhee, *The French Revolution 1789-1799* (Oxford 2002) and P.M. Jones *The French Revolution 1787-1804* second edition (London, 2010). Malcolm Crook (ed.) *Revolutionary France 1788-1880* (Oxford, 2002) is strong on longer-term repercussions, as is D.M.G. Sutherland, *The French Revolution and Empire; the quest for a civic order* (Oxford, 2003).

Origins:
William Doyle, *Origins of the French Revolution* third edition (Oxford 1999) is an essential discussion of the evolution of historiography on

this topic from the mid-20th century to the 1989 bicentenary. Peter R. Campbell (ed.) *The Origins of the French Revolution* (Basingstoke, 2006) updates this with more recent scholarship.

Overview Collections:

Several very wide-ranging collections of essays have recently been produced: David Andress (ed.) *The Oxford Handbook of the French Resvolution* (Oxford, 2015); Peter McPhee (ed.) A *Companion to the French Revolution* (Oxford, 2013), and Alan Forrest & Matthias Middell (ed.) *The Routledge Companion to the French Revolution in World History* (London, 2015).

Controversy:

For a full-throated denunciation of the Revolution, one can still read Simon Schama, *Citizens; a chronicle of the French Revolution* (London, 1989), while Keith Michael Baker, *Inventing the French Revolution* (Cambridge, 1990) gives a more intellectual gloss to the problem. Against them, very directly and explicitly, in brief there is Sophie Wahnich, *In Defence of the Terror: Liberty or Death in the French Revolution* (London, 2012) and at greater length Eric Hazan, *A People's History of the French Revolution* (London, 2014).

The Early Revolution:

Timothy Tackett, *Becoming a Revolutionary; the Deputies of the French National Assembly and the*

Emergence of a Revolutionary Culture (1789–1790) (Princeton, 1996) remains a landmark study of the transition from pre-revolutionary to revolutionary attitudes. Michael P. Fitzsimmons, *The Remaking of France: The National Assembly and the Constitution of 1791* (Cambridge, 1994) attempts to portray the positive dimensions of the political process that unfolded from 1789. Timothy Tackett, *When the King Took Flight* (Cambridge, MA, 2003), shows what happened when royal escape shattered any prospect of constitutional consensus.

Into the Terror:
Timothy Tackett's most recent work, *The Coming of the Terror in the French Revolution* (Cambridge, MA, 2015) is an interesting attempt to portray events in detail drawing on the accounts of eyewitnesses. For a wider view, there remains David Andress, *The Terror; civil war in the French Revolution* (London, 2005), and *The French Revolution and the People* (London, 2004). On Robespierre and his role, two contrasting biographical approaches are Ruth Scurr, *Fatal Purity; Robespierre and the French Revolution* (London, 2006) and Peter McPhee, *Robespierre; a revolutionary life*, (New Haven, 2012). Marisa Linton, *Choosing Terror; virtue, friendship and authenticity in the French Revolution* (Oxford, 2013) examines the close interactions and beliefs of the circle of leaders at the heart of the Terror. Perhaps the most stimulating view of wider

Parisian radical politics under the Terror is Morris Slavin, *The Hébertistes to the Guillotine: anatomy of a 'conspiracy' in revolutionary France* (Baton Rouge, 1994). Jean-Pierre Gross, *Fair Shares For All: Jacobin Egalitarianism in Practice* (Cambridge, 1997) makes the case for the Terror not having been so 'terrible' always or everywhere.

After the Terror:
Bronislaw Baczko, *Ending the Terror; the French Revolution after Robespierre* (Cambridge, 1994) remains the essential study of Thermidorian politics. Howard G. Brown, *Ending the French Revolution; violence, justice and repression from the Terror to Napoleon* (Charlottesville, 2006) is a similarly essential overview of the emergence of authoritarian solutions to political problems in the later 1790s. Andrew Jainchill, *Reimagining Politics after the Terror: The Republican Origins of French Liberalism* (Ithaca, 2008) explores the impact of this on the sphere of political ideas.

War:
T.C.W. Blanning, *The Origins of the French Revolutionary Wars* (Routledge, 1986) and *The French Revolutionary Wars 1787-1802* (London, 1996) remain excellent overviews. David A. Bell, *The First Total War: Napoleon's Europe and the Birth of Modern Warfare* (London, 2007), despite its title, contains an important discussion of how attitudes to war, and the perception of opponents

as enemies, rather than mere rivals, changed critically in the 1790s.

Global Dimensions:
Bailey Stone, *Reinterpreting the French Revolution; a global-historical perspective* (Cambridge, 2002) places the Revolution in a context of great-power diplomacy and imperial rivalry, seen from the "top down". Suzanne Desan, Lynn Hunt and William Max Nelson (ed.) *The French Revolution in Global Perspective* (Ithaca, 2013) treat the "global" dimension from a more bottom-up approach. Wim Klooster, *Revolutions in the Atlantic World; a comparative history* (New York, 2009) and Lloyd Kramer, *Nationalism in Europe & America; politics, cultures and identities since 1775* (Chapel Hill, 2011) are explicitly comparative studies, while David Armitage and Sanjay Subrahmanyan (ed.) *The Age of Revolutions in Global Context* (Basingstoke, 2010) picks up broader themes, and Christophe Belaubre, Jordana Dym and John Savage (ed.) *Napoleon's Atlantic; the impact of Napoleonic empire in the Atlantic world* (Leiden, 2010) extend discussion into the 19th century.

Caribbean Revolution:
This has become a major research topic in its own right in recent decades, led by works such as Carolyn E. Fick, *The Making of Haiti: The Saint Domingue Revolution From Below* (Knoxville, 1990). Laurent Dubois, *A Colony of Citizens:*

Revolution and Slave Emancipation in the French Caribbean, 1787-1804 (Chapel Hill, 2004), and *Avengers of the New World: The Story of the Haitian Revolution* (Cambridge, MA, 2004), was among those instrumental in taking this evolution to a new stage, which has been followed by an explosion of work. Much of this is documented in Jeremy D. Popkin, *A Concise History of the Haitian Revolution* (Malden, 2012); see also Malick Ghachem, *The Old Regime and the Haitian Revolution* (New York, 2011).

Fiction and Film:

Hilary Mantel, *A Place of Greater Safety* (first published 1992) is probably the most evocative novel of the Revolution for the modern reader, though historians should of course be wary of how much of her subjects' inner life and background she has made up, however plausibly. Anatole France, *The Gods Will Have Blood* (first published 1912) is a much earlier attempt to imaginatively reconstruct the experience of the Terror for 'ordinary' individuals caught up in it, while remaining more approachable than heavyweight 19th-century fictions – Dickens' *Tale of Two Cities*, Victor Hugo's *1793* (and of course NOT *Les Misérables*, which is about the 1830s), or the many works of Balzac that dissect post-revolutionary society, its secrets and vendettas.

On the screen, Sophia Coppola's *Marie Antoinette*

(2006) is not a realistic depiction, but it is an effective impression of a life of aristocratic frivolity and excess. The 2001 film *The Affair of the Necklace* gives some insight into the machinations of court life in the 1780s, though it is not the most entertaining watch. *Ridicule* (1996) is a French-language production set around less specific real-life events, but very successfully conveying the spirit of the aristocratic court, and revulsion against it. The classic 1982 French film *La Nuit de Varennes* is similarly effective for events around the 1791 royal flight. *The Lady and the Duke* (2001) portrays, in a somewhat stylised fashion, the evolution of Parisian politics towards the Terror, seen through the eyes of a British woman romantically involved with the king's cousin.

For sheer screen impact, it remains difficult to beat Andrzej Wajda's 1983 film of *Danton*, with Gérard Depardieu giving a barnstorming performance as the title-character, tense undertones of the politics of Soviet-era Poland, and (literally) buckets of blood.

It is now possible to walk through the streets of revolutionary Paris in the video-game Assassins Creed Unity. This is an impressive visual recreation of the architecture of the city, achieved with a board of academic advisors, but due to the demands of the underlying fantasy plot, nothing the game tells you about "historical" characters can be relied on.

INDEX

A

Alpaugh, Micah 89
American Declaration of Independence 43, 45, 67
American War of Independence 1, 15, 23, 41–43, 45, 125
Aristocracy 3, 31–32, 41–43, 49–51, 105
  émigrés 3, 4, 54, 62
  salons, and Parisian culture 36–38
  Second Estate, of Nobles 2, 27, 43, 47–48, 126
  Society of Thirty 43–45, 48
  see also Counter-revolution
Artois, Charles Philippe, Count of 54
Assembly of Notables 1, 25–26, 28, 40–42
Assignats (monetary bonds) 57, 61–62, 68
Austria, war with France 4–5, 11–13, 46, 109, 113
Avignon, annexation 61

B

Barras, Paul 104–105, 107, 109
Barruel, Abbé Augustin
  History of Jacobinism 16
Barry, Jeanne Bécu, Madame du 34
Bastille
  book hoard in 38, 67, 79
  storming of 2, 51, 52
Beauharnais, Joséphine de 105
Belgium, annexation 78, 109, 113
Boilly, Louis Léopold
  portrait of Simon Chenard 82
Bonaparte, Napoleon 12–14, 74, 87, 103, 105, 108–115, 112
Book trade, illegal 37–39, 65, 67–68
Brienne, Loménie de 25–27
Brissot, Jacques-Pierre 4, 62, 63–64
Brissotins 4–8, 62, 64, 81, 125
  see also Girondins
Brown, Howard 108
Burke, Edmund
  Reflections on the Revolution in France 15, 18
Burrows, Simon 37–38

C

Cahiers de doléances ("registers of grievance") 45–47, 65
Calonne, Charles Alexandre de 1, 24–25, 40–41
Camp de Jalès (Catholic march) 57–58
Capitalism 17, 19–20
Caribbean slave colonies, French 20, 23, 116–117
Carlyle, Thomas 93
Carnot, Lazare 104, 107
Catholic Church 3, 13, 16, 27–30, 33, 41, 56–59, 61
  and the First Estate 2, 27–28, 41, 46–47, 126
Chabord, Joseph
  portrait of Napoleon I 112
Charles I of England, King 23
Chenard, Simon 82
Clay, Lauren 20
Clubs (political groups) 12, 55, 75–78
Cobb, Richard 117
Colonies, French colonial 20, 23,

116–117
Committee of Public Safety 7, 78, 93, 100, 104, 125
Communism 17
Convention *see* National Assembly
Cordeliers (political club) 76, 77
Counter-revolution 3, 5, 7, 53–57, 60–63, 80, 86
    see also Vendée revolt

D
Danton, Georges Jacques 77–78, 90, 92–93
Darnton, Robert 37
De Baumarchais, Pierre Augustin Caron
    The Marriage of Figaro 38
Declaration of the Rights of Man and the Citizen, National Convention 3, 28, 43, 45, 53–54, 67, 70
Desan, Suzanne 119
Dickens, Charles
    Tale of Two Cities 16
Directory 12, 14, 103–108, 114, 127
Drouais, François-Hubert
    portrait of Madame du Barry 34

E
Economic crises, pre-revolution 1, 13, 23–29, 61–62, 64, 106
    assignats (monetary bonds) 57, 61–62, 68
tax reform attempts 23–26, 29–31, 41
Egypt, Bonaparte's expedition to 13–14, 111–113, 116–117
Émigrés, French aristocracy 3, 4, 54, 62
Enlightenment 16, 22, 27, 29–30, 36, 119, 126
Enragés (female radicals) 72–73

Estates-General 1–2, 25–28, 41–49, 67–68, 114, 126
    Cahiers de doléances ("registers of grievance") 45–47, 65

F
"Fallen Idols" Nos.1-3: 45–46, 63–64, 77–78
First Estate, of Catholic clergy 2, 27–28, 41, 46–47, 126
Freemasonry 16, 126
French Revolution
    as attack on religion 56–59
    causes, social and political 19–25
    and censorship 32–40, 65, 106
    and class mobility 19–21, 27–28, 32–35, 51, 88–89
    counter-revolution 3, 5, 7, 53–57, 60–63, 80, 86
    crowd violence 88–91
    economic crises, pre-revolution 1, 13, 23–29, 61–62, 64, 106
    historical criticism and legacy 15–19, 115–121
    images 52, 70, 82
    key terms 125–128
    political culture of 32–35, 60–66, 71–78
    political language, extreme 78–83
    political violence 54–56
    popular uprisings of 1789, significance 48–53
    after Robespierre's death 98–103
    social reform attempts, pre-revolution 23–35, 29–31, 41
    ten facts about 67–69
    timeline 1–14
    and women 68, 71–74, 121
    see also Terror

Furet, François 17

G
General Maximum, The (1793) 7, 11, 128
George III of the United Kingdom, King 23
Girondins 5–8, 64, 71–72, 77, 90, 93, 96, 125
   see also Brissotins
Gouges, Olympe de 71–72
Grenoble ("Day of Tiles") 26
Gruder, Vivian 30
Guillotine 85–88, 91, 96–99

H
Hardman, John 30, 94–95
Hébert, Jacques-René 83–84
Hugo, Victor
   Les Misérables 92

J
Italy, war with France 6, 11–13, 109–110, 113

J
Jacobin movement
   and Brissot, Jacques-Pierre 63–64
   definition 126
   founding of 16, 40, 75–78
   and Lafayette, Marquis de 46
   neo-Jacobin movement 114
   and Robespierre 95
   after Robespierre/Terror 100, 103
   see also Montagnards
Jefferson, Thomas 45, 50, 67
Jones, Colin 20
Jones, P.M. 41
Jourdan Law (1798), on conscription 111, 113

L
Lacombe, Claire 72–73
Lafayette, Marquis de 42–43, 45–46, 51, 59, 67, 80
Law of 22 Prairial (1794) 95, 100, 126–127
Law of Two-Thirds (1975) 12, 102–103
Legislative Assembly 4, 46, 62–64, 81, 93
Léon, Pauline 72–73
Lettres de cachet ("letters under seal") 33–34, 39
Lilti, Antoine 36–37
Louis XV, King of France 23–24, 39, 79
Louis XVI of France, King
   "Flight to Varennes," and capture 4, 28–29, 56, 60–61, 63, 68
   mistress, Madame du Barry 34
   and National Assembly 2, 28, 48, 54–55
   personal perspective 27–30
   and pre-revolution social change 22–26, 38
   relationship with Marie Antoinette 27–29, 67
   trial and execution 6, 30
Louis XVII of France 102
Louis XVIII of France, King 102
Lucas, Colin 20

M
McPhee, Peter 95
Marat, Jean-Paul 60, 64, 68–69, 80
Marie Antoinette, Queen of France 8, 27–29, 38, 46, 56, 67, 79
Marriage of Figaro, The, de Baumarchais, Pierre Augustin Caron 38
Marx, Karl, and Marxism 17, 88

Mass Levy 7, 96, 127
Montagnards 5–9, 64, 72–73, 77–78, 81, 101, 120, 127

N

Napoleon Bonaparte 12–14, 74, 87, 103, 105, 108–115, 112
Napoleonic Code (1804) 119
National Assembly
  assignats (monetary bonds) 57, 61–62, 68
  Committee of Public Safety 7, 78, 93, 100, 104, 125
  Declaration of the Rights of Man and the Citizen 3, 28, 43, 45, 53–54, 67, 70
  definition 127
  early revolutionary culture 55–66
  Law of 22 Prairial (1794) 95, 100, 126–127
  and Louis XVI of France, King 2, 28, 48, 54–55
  and popular uprisings of 1789, 48–53
  Revolutionary Tribunal 6, 8, 69, 78, 85–86, 95–96
  and Robespierre 93–94, 100
  timeline 2–9, 11–13
  violent language of 79–80
National Guard 45, 51, 58–59, 61
Necker, Jacques 23, 27–28, 41, 43–44, 48
Netherlands, France's occupation of 11, 109, 113
Nicholas II of Russia, King 23
"Night of 4 August" (1789) 68
Nîmes, *Bagarre de Nîmes* (street violence) 57–58
Nobility *see* Aristocracy

P

Paine, Thomas
  Rights of Man 15
Parlements (appellate courts) 21–28, 30–33, 39, 48, 72
Police, la (authorities), censorship and control 34–35
Press, freedom and censorship 3, 20, 32–35, 65–66, 69, 79–80, 106
Provincial Assemblies 41–42
Prussia, war with France 5, 11, 109

R

Revolutionary Tribunal 6, 8, 69, 78, 85–86, 95–96
Robespierre, Maximilien 4, 7, 9–11, 10, 40, 64, 69, 78, 91–100
Roland, Manon 72
Rousseau, Jean-Jacques 39–40, 81
Rudé, George 88

S

Salons, and Parisian aristocracy 36–38
Sans-culottes (common people/radicals) 6–11, 18–19, 82, 83–84, 90, 127
Schama, Simon
  Citizens 18, 88, 98
Seaward, Louise 38
Second Assembly of Notables 28
Second Estate, of Nobles 2, 27, 43, 47–48, 126
September Massacres (1792) 77, 90
Seven Years' War 1, 127–128
Sieyès, Abbé
  What is the Third Estate? 44–45, 114
Society of Thirty 43–45, 48
Sonenscher, Michael 83
Spain, war with France 6, 11, 109

T

Tackett, Timothy 20–21, 44–45, 47–48
Taine, Hippolyte 16
Tax reform, pre-revolution attempts 23–26, 29–31, 41
Terror
  crowd violence 88–91
  events 96–100
  executions during 9, 85–88
  historical criticism 18, 119
  political system behind 6, 8–9
  Revolutionary Tribunal 6, 8, 69, 78, 85–86, 95–96
  White Terror 102
Thermidor 9, 69, 95, 99, 101–103, 122, 128
Third Estate 2, 28, 43–44, 47–48, 67–68, 114, 126
  see also National Assembly
Tocqueville, Alexis de 46–47
Tuileries Palace, Paris 59, 65–66, 92
Turgot, Anne Robert Jacques 24

U

United Kingdom
  free trade treaty with France 49
  views on French Revolution 15–16
  war with France 6, 11, 12–13, 111–114

V

Valmy, Prussian defeat at 5
Varennes, "Flight to Varennes" 4, 56, 60–61, 63, 68
Vendée revolt 6–8, 59, 73–74, 87, 118
Versailles
  Estates-General meeting at 2, 47–48
  "March on Versailles" 54–55

W

Walton, Charles 78
White Terror 102
Woloch, Isser 114–115
Women 68, 71–74, 121

First published in 2016 by
Connell Guides
Artist House
35 Little Russell Street
London WC1A 2HH

10 9 8 7 6 5 4 3 2 1

Copyright © Connell Guides Publishing Ltd.
All rights reserved. No part of this publication
may be reproduced, stored in a retrieval system or transmitted in any
form, or by any means (electronic, mechanical, or otherwise) without
the prior written permission of both the copyright owners
and the publisher.

Picture credits:
p.52 © Design Pics Inc/Rex/Shutterstock
p.82 © Design Pics Inc/Rex/Shutterstock
p.112 © Getty Images

A CIP catalogue record for this book is available from the British Library.
ISBN 978-1-907776-82-3

Edited by Jolyon Connell and Anna Neima

Design © Nathan Burton
Assistant Editors & typeset by
Paul Woodward & Holly Bruce

www.connellguides.com